Modernist Cooking Made Easy:
A Beginner's Guide to Ingredients, Techniques, and Recipes

A special edition of
Modernist Cooking Made Easy: Getting Started

By Jason Logsdon

ISBN-13: 978-1483933436

ISBN-10: 1483933431

For my wonderful wife,
who continues to support everything I do,
no matter how crazy.

TABLE OF CONTENTS

PREFACE

When Chris Anderson from Modernist Pantry approached me about releasing a special edition of *Modernist Cooking Made Easy: Getting Started* I was thrilled. I've been using ingredients from Modernist Pantry for a few years and I love their customer service. They are also approachable both to the home cook and the professional chef, which makes them a great fit for what we are trying to accomplish with Modernist Cooking Made Easy.

We hope you enjoy this special edition of *Modernist Cooking Made Easy: Getting Started* and have great success in the kitchen.

Jason Logsdon
www.ModernistCookingMadeEasy.com

FOREWORD

By Chris Anderson

My journey into the world of Modernist Cooking began several years ago when it was hard to find both information and the ingredients necessary to explore this exciting new type of cuisine. Janie and I were living in Manhattan and were caught up in its incredible restaurant scene. I was also working to advance my cooking skills by attending evening classes at the top culinary schools in the city. During one of these evenings at the French Culinary Institute, I met Dave Arnold, the FCI Director of Culinary Technology, and was introduced to an immersion circulator and sous vide cooking for the first time. Needless to say, I was immediately hooked.

As a software developer for over 20 years, I have a natural affinity for science and technology. As someone with a lifelong passion for food, I've been intrigued by the relationship between science and cooking ever since I read the first edition of Harold McGee's, On Food and Cooking. I really appreciate the work of educators like Harold and Alton Brown, who focus not just on what to do in the kitchen but why.

So I spent the next few weeks googling everything I could find on what was then known as "molecular gastronomy". Most of the information available was about famous chefs who were pioneers of this new wave; Jose Andres, Heston Blumenthal, Grant Achatz, Wylie Dufresne, and of course Ferran Adria.

The next logical step was a visit to WD-50, where Wylie and his pastry chef Alex Stupak treated us to one of the most unique and interesting meals I've ever experienced.

Although the task seemed daunting, I knew that I had to try and recreate some of the magic of these dishes at home. The first problem that I ran into was the limited amount of information available on the ingredients and techniques that were required to pull off most of these dishes. And when I did manage to piece together enough info to make a go, it was impossible (even in NYC) to find some of the exotic ingredients that I needed. I ended up having to mail order kilos of powders with strange sounding names like transglutaminase, iota carrageenan and xanthan gum. And subsequently spent many late nights creating a mess in our kitchenette with my experiments.

If you've ever lived in Manhattan or any large city, you'll understand that there's a premium on space (especially kitchen space). So it was no surprise that my new passion quickly became a source of tension between me and the love of my life, Janie. Fortunately the story has a happy ending. The experience led to what is now Modernist Pantry, a one-stop source for both home cooks and professional chefs, who are interested in discovering the secrets of Modernist Cooking. We also ended up moving to a large house on the Maine seacoast, with no shortage of kitchen or storage space.

I only wish that I had a book, like the one you are holding in your hand, from the beginning. It would have saved me countless hours of trial and error, not to mention aggravation. Jason Logsdon has done an extraordinary job of presenting these essential Modernist techniques in a way that's easy to understand, especially for those of us who are not professionally trained chefs.

Of course you could go out and buy Modernist Cuisine, the magnum opus by Nathan Myhrvold, Chris Young and Maxim Billet, which I highly recommend as the ultimate guide to Modernist Cooking. But if you aren't quite ready to shell out $600 for a cookbook, Modernist Cooking Made Easy provides an affordable yet comprehensive introduction to the subject.

SECTION ONE

INTRODUCTION TO MODERNIST COOKING

ACKNOWLEDGMENTS

In cooking, most new dishes, flavors, and techniques are building on the work of prior generations of cooks. There are very few truly original works and we all owe a debt of gratitude to those that came before us and paved the way for us. There has been a great tradition of sharing and codifying cooking techniques from Escoffier to Ferran Adrià to Grant Achatz to Nathan Myhrvold, each of which built on the works of those that came before.

This book is no exception. I could never have written it, much less explored the latest modernist techniques, without the chefs, authors, and cooks who experimented with food, and most importantly, shared their knowledge with us in books and on the internet.

I'd especially like to mention several resources that were invaluable in creating this book. I highly recommend them for you to read if you want more in-depth knowledge.

Alinea by Grant Achatz is filled with amazing techniques and whimsical dishes. Aki Kamozawa and H. Alexander Talbot delve into the "why" in their *Ideas in Food* book, as well as their always informative website. *Texture - A hydrocolloid recipe collection*, compiled by Martin Lersch from Khymos.com, is a great compendium of recipes for many modernist ingredients. The *Hydrocolloids Primer* from Dave Arnold and the Cooking Issues website help to clarify some of the uses of and reasons for modernist ingredients . And, of course, the comprehensive *Modernist Cuisine* by Nathan Myhrvold, which covers pretty much every cooking technique you would ever need to know.

All of these resources gave me a foundation that I could use to explore the techniques and ingredients found in this book.

How To Use This Book

This book is meant to be used as both a reference guide and instruction manual for the new techniques and ingredients that are being used in modernist cooking. It has been written so each chapter can be used independently. I do recommend reading the Introduction to Modernist Cooking section first since it will provide you with a foundation of knowledge required to understand the remainder of the chapters.

After you have read the introduction chapters, there is no need to read the book straight through unless you want to. Feel free to jump around to any of the techniques or ingredients that interest you. If you seek additional information about a recipe you can look up the specific ingredients or techniques used in it to get a more detailed description of how they work.

We have provided images of many of the dishes. For larger, full color images you can go to:

www.modernistcookingmadeeasy.com/getting-started

To stay up to date with modernist cooking and what we are working on you can:

Join our monthly newsletter at: http://eepurl.com/owpNb

Follow me on twitter at: @jasonlogsdon_sv

Like our Facebook page at: www.facebook.com/ModernistCookingMadeEasy

Most importantly of all, remember to have fun!

WHAT IS MODERNIST COOKING?

If you have any questions you can ask them in the Modernist Cooking Forums on our website. Just post your question and other cooks will weigh in with their answers.

You can find them on our website at:
www.modernistcookingmadeeasy.com/modernist-cooking-forums

Modernist cooking goes by many names including avant-garde, **modernist** cuisine, haute cuisine, and molecular gastronomy. In general, these terms really just mean any cooking that uses the most modern techniques. They tend to be associated with the more refined plating style and the use of esoteric ingredients but they really encompass all cooking knowledge.

The focus of this book is on the newer, modernist techniques and ingredients.

ARE THESE CHEMICALS SAFE?

One of the most common questions I get asked is some variation of "are these chemicals safe" or "why do you use these chemicals? I prefer natural foods".

I have to be honest, these are also questions that I asked myself before I started embracing molecular gastronomy. When I began looking for answers, what I found was pretty amazing. These "new chemicals" are really no different than many of the ingredients we currently use in cooking and many of them have been around for a long, long time.

For instance, agar has been used in Asian cooking for hundreds of years and is just the extract from a certain type of algae. Xanthan gum is produced by fermenting sugar with a certain bacteria found in cabbage.

Unless you are on a "raw" or "paleo" diet, these ingredients are no more processed than kitchen stables you typically eat at home. Cornstarch (steeped, fermented, ground, washed, centrifuged, and dried corn)[1] and sugar (diffused, clarified with lime, heated, evaporated, ionized, seeded, centrifuged, then dried sugarcane or beets)[2] aren't exactly pure, not to mention common

ingredients like baking soda (sodium bicarbonate, a reaction of sodium chloride, ammonia, and carbon dioxide).

I'm not a scientist or a nutritionist, but it seems to me if you bake, thicken liquids with cornstarch, or eat anything with sugar in it, then you shouldn't have any issues with using the majority of the modernist ingredients. Many of these modernist ingredients are also used in normal store-bought foods such as sandwich bread, mayonnaise, ice cream, and salad dressings and have been for decades.

SCIENCE OR COOKING?

A major criticism of molecular gastronomy is that it is "science" not "cooking", and that you need to understand chemistry and have lots of fancy equipment.

I think this viewpoint is mainly due to how recently many of these ingredients have started to be used in American kitchens. Because of this, there has been a lot of experimentation and explanation about how they work. All of this discussion took place for our traditional ingredients centuries ago, but these exact same discussions did occur.

For instance, you need to add water to the powdered mix and whisk until the thickening agent is evenly dispersed, becomes hydrated and a thick foam is formed, leavened by the carbon dioxide produced by the $NaHCO_3$ interacting with the hydrogen. The foam is then heated over medium-high heat until the cellular foam structure solidifies and sets, and non-enzymatic browning covers the surface.

Or, you could say "add water to the instant pancake mix, stir together, and cook until it isn't wet and the outside browns."

This same idea applies to molecular gastronomy too. To utilize the thickening power of xanthan gum you don't need to understand how it works on a molecular level, just that adding some to a liquid will cause it to thicken.

I'm willing to bet that the majority of the people who say molecular gastronomy is too complicated can make instant pancake mix just fine but couldn't begin to tell you how it works.

DO I NEED LAB EQUIPMENT?

Similar to the last point, many people picture fancy, expensive equipment in a sterile lab. The truth is that the majority of modernist cooking can be done with standard kitchen tools you already have on hand.

In the Equipment section we give our recommendation for "required" modernist equipment and the total cost is under $100.

Sure, things like rotary evaporators and centrifuges cost thousands of dollars but they are equipment used for very specific purposes and most cooks would never need them.

WHY DO PEOPLE FEEL THIS WAY?

There are many reasons that people have these misconceptions but I think the biggest one is very simple:

Clear, concise information for the average cook isn't easily available.

This book aims to change that by providing you with a base of knowledge that you can apply to your own cooking.

WHAT MAKES A MODERNIST DISH?

Many modernist dishes are based on traditional foods that have been tweaked in one of several ways. The dish may maintain the same flavor profile, though it doesn't have to, but the change in texture, size, and use will result in a dish all of its own.

A NON-MODERNIST EXAMPLE

A great example of taking two dishes that have the same components but are different dishes is for New England Clam Chowder. You can eat it in a nice restaurant, in a white bowl, with small oyster crackers floating on top.
In casual restaurants this dish is often re-imagined as a ladle of clam chowder in a hollowed out bread bowl.
The soup itself may be unchanged but changing the bread component from a small, hard, floating garnish to a large, soft, serving vessel creates an entirely new dish.

Change the Size

Modernist dishes tend to be on the smaller side. Taking an existing dish and making the components smaller is a great way to make something new. Some modernist techniques can help you with this but they aren't needed for many transformations. For instance, you can reduce sauces or just cut proteins into bite-size pieces, or just focus on keeping the serving size small. Of course, you can also create small films or gels to shrink the size of liquids.

Conversely, taking something small and making it bigger can also reinvent a dish. For liquid components using a foam is a great way to increase the size without increasing the actual amount of the ingredient.

Change the Texture

Changing textures is a staple of modernist dishes. Changing the texture not only affects the flavor of the food, but also how it feels in your mouth and its appearance.

Using the techniques and ingredients laid out in this book makes it very easy to change the texture of your dishes. Liquids can be thickened or turned into foams. Turning oils into powders is a great way to change up the texture of a dish.

Gels and films are a unique way to present ingredients that would traditionally be liquids. Is there a component you can puree, foam, and then dehydrate?

Change the Use of an Ingredient

Is there an accent ingredient that can be made into the star of the dish? People have been doing this for centuries, from the soup in a bread bowl to Korean BBQ wrapped in lettuce leaves.

MODERNIST COOKING BASICS

If you need more information about a specific modernist cooking term, technique, or ingredient, you can check out our modernist glossary at:

www.modernistcookingmadeeasy.com/info/
molecular-gastronomy-glossary

Modernist cooking is a very broad term that encompasses most of cooking. In this book we are focusing on a subset of modernist cooking dealing with many of the new techniques and ingredients available to us. In order to understand how to use these new tools there are a few things to learn first.

COMMON TERMS

There are a few concepts used in modernist cooking, and actually in all cooking, that are critical to understanding how the recipes will work.

Dispersion

Dispersion refers to the process of evenly distributing one ingredient into another one. Proper dispersion is critical to ensure the ingredient affects all of the mixture it is going into instead of forming clumps.

Different ingredients are dispersed in different ways, and the most effective way will be discussed in the chapter on that ingredient. For instance, sugar is easily dispersed in hot water while flour will form clumps.

Hydration

Many of the ingredients need to be hydrated before they will work. Hydration is simply the process of adding water to the ingredient. You also often need to bring the liquid to a specific temperature to ensure the ingredient will hydrate properly. For instance, after you add flour to water to make a gravy you have to heat it up before the flour will thicken it.

This is also true of many baking preparations, such as letting popover dough sit for 30 minutes for the flour to fully hydrate.

Ingredient Ratios

Many of the ingredients will specify the ratio they should be used in. All the ratios refer to the weights of the ingredients. For example, an agar recipe might say to add 2% agar. The 2% means that the weight of the agar should be 2% of the weight of the liquid it is being added to. So if you had 300 grams of fruit juice you would add 6 grams of agar to it, or 300 x 0.02.

Viscosity

Viscosity is the "resistance to flow" that a liquid possesses. At its most basic this just measures how easy something is to pour. Water has a low viscosity and maple syrup, especially cold out of the refrigerator, has a high viscosity.

Many of the ingredients in this book can thicken liquids and increase their viscosity.

EXACTNESS IN MEASURING

There are two contradictory thoughts about modernist cooking and using some of the very powerful ingredients.

The first thought is that everything must be very precisely measured and the recipes must be followed to the letter.

The second thought is that ingredients from different companies will have different strengths and the quantities may have to be adjusted, especially if the recipe doesn't specify an exact brand.

Both of these statements are true and come into play depending on what you are trying to accomplish.

However, this is nothing new since both of these statements are true for traditional cooking as well. Unbleached flour from King Arthur will thicken gravy, make cakes, and form pie crusts differently than Gold Medal unbleached flour, much less their Gold Medal cake flour. A recipe calling for a "large tomato" leaves a lot of room for what size that actually is.

As home cooks we have learned to live with those differences and accept that our dish might not turn out exactly the same as the dish from the recipe, and no one will notice. For chefs, however, reproducing the exact same dish is of the utmost importance so these nuances really come into play.

I think because modernist cooking is mainly being practiced in restaurants by talented chefs there has been an emphasis on exact measurements that is very intimidating to the home cook. While the exactness is required in restaurant kitchens, home cooks can afford to be much looser.

Yes, you probably need a scale to measure grams, but this is mainly because the quantities are so small. I could adapt the recipes to call for 1/32 of a teaspoon, but most home cooks wouldn't have one. This makes measuring by weight very effective.

Also, since the ingredients interact with the particles in each other, the volume begins to become less important than the mass, expressed by weight.

Many of the ingredients are also powders and can have very different volumes based on how they have been stored. Michael Ruhlman pointed out that a cup of flour can weigh between 4 and 6 ounces, a 50% difference, depending on how packed it is.

All of these reasons highlight why we use scales and weight measurements instead of volume measurements. Plus, there's no measuring cups to clean!

Remember though, just because you have precision at your fingertips doesn't mean you have to obsess over it. All of the recipes in this book provide gram measurements for most ingredients, but use common sense when measuring them. If you are within 1-2% of the correct weight of any ingredient then it should be fine. For 500 grams of water, about 2 cups, that is a 5 to 10 gram difference. For 3.2 grams of agar that is a 0.03 to 0.06 gram swing.

Proper Weighing

To someone not familiar with using a scale it can be a little intimidating until you use it once or twice. The main concept of using the scale is the learning to "tare" or "zero" the scale. All digital scales will have a "tare" / "zero" button. What this does is reset the weight to zero.

This allows you to measure all the ingredients in the same bowl. You simply turn on the scale and place the bowl on it. Hit the tare button so it resets to zero. Add the next ingredient, then tare it to zero again. Repeat for all the ingredients.

You will most likely have to use a larger scale for the liquids or main ingredients and a gram scale for the modernist ingredients.

Common Flavored Liquids

Part of the fun with modernist cooking is experimenting with different flavors. Many of the techniques start out with a flavored liquid. Here are some common sources of liquids that can be turned into foams, airs, and gels to get you started.

Citrus Juices

Most citrus juices work well as airs and light foams. You may want to add some sugar or water to help balance out the flavors.

Pre-Made Sauces

Most pantries contain many pre-made, strong sauces that work great as light foams or gels. Soy sauce, mirin, or fish sauce components are great on Asian-inspired dishes. Worcester sauce, steak sauce, and thin vinegar-based BBQ sauce based components add texture and flavor to steak, pork, and chicken.

Vinegars

Vinegar is often used in a dish or sauce to add brightness and acidity. You can take that same concept but use the vinegar to create a flavorful component to also add visual appeal to the dish. You may want to add some sugar or water to the vinegar to balance the flavor if it is too strong.

Vegetable and Fruit Juices

For a more subtle, yet just as interesting take you can use vegetable or fruit juices. If you have a juicer or good blender you can make your own, otherwise many grocery stores sell a variety of natural juices. If there are lots of particles in the juice then be sure to strain it through a chinois or cheesecloth if you want a more refined presentation.

These components can be added to traditional dishes for a dramatic flavor and visual effect. Some great pairings are apple cider on pork chops, carrot on peas and pancetta, or a cranberry on turkey.

Brewed Liquids

Coffees and teas open up a wide range of liquids and flavors you can use in your dishes. Brew the coffee or tea then you can turn it into a foam or gel and add it to dishes. From the whimsical, like orange-peppermint air on cake, to the hearty, like french roast coffee pudding on steak, you have many interesting options.

For another take on teas, you can create your own tea by steeping herbs, spices, and aromatics in hot water. I really enjoy thyme and rosemary air on pork, juniper and thyme foam on duck, or orange peel and fennel fluid gel on salmon.

MODERNIST EQUIPMENT

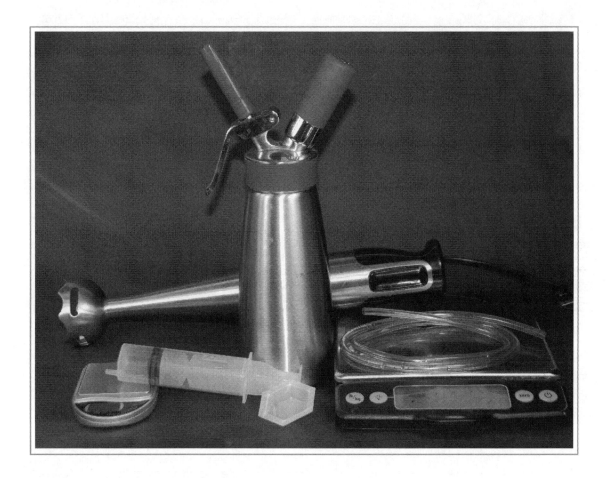

We are continually adding and reviewing modernist equipment as it becomes available.

You can find them on our website at:
www.modernistcookingmadeeasy.com/info/
modernist-equipment

Modernist cooking can use a wide variety of equipment and tools. Many of them have very specific uses and are only used for advanced techniques. We want to focus on the more accessible equipment, most of which can be used in traditional cooking as well.

Most of the equipment in this section can be found on Amazon.com but we also have a list of other sources in our Ingredient and Tool Sources section in the references.

STARTING EQUIPMENT

There are many different tools and pieces of equipment that modernist chefs use. These range from $5 tweezers used in plating to $10,000 rotary evaporators. Even with all this variety, someone getting started can get by with just four items, costing under $100 combined.

Then, depending on your interests you can invest some money in different sections of molecular gastronomy, though almost every technique covered in this book can be done with very inexpensive tools.

There are also a few kits available that come with many of the modernist ingredients as well as some standard tools. I have used the Cuisine R-Evolution kit from Molecular-R and it comes with a good variety of tools and ingredients for about $60.

Required Equipment
Gram scale, $10-20
Kilogram / pound scale, $10-20
Immersion blender, $30-60
Whisk, $6-10

Helpful Items
Weighing dishes, $1-2

Hemispherical or spherical molds, $10-20
Plastic or silicon molds, $10-20
Acetate sheets, $5-10
Plastic syringe and tubing, $8-12
Spherification syringe, $3-6
Rapid caviar maker, $50-60
Caviar / sphere strainer, $5-10
Chinois, $35-70

Big Ticket Equipment
Heat resistant whipping siphon, $100-120
Standing blender, $30-100
Sous vide machine, $150-800
Juicer, $50-350
Dehydrator, $30-90
Standing mixer, with whisk attachment
    $100-300

REQUIRED EQUIPMENT

The only equipment really needed for the majority of the recipes and techniques in this book are a gram scale, a kilogram scale, an immersion blender, and a whisk. Most everything else you probably already have on hand in your kitchen.

Scales

There are two types of scales needed for most modernist cooking. A gram scale, for weighing out small ingredients and a kilogram / pound scale, for measuring large amounts of an ingredient.

I recommend electronic versions of each scale, they tend to be much more accurate and allow you to easily tare (reset) the scale so you can just add ingredients into the same bowl.

The kilogram / pound scales typically increase in increments of 1 gram which works well. A maximum weight of at least 2,250 grams / 5 pounds is ideal, and I prefer one with at least 10 pounds so I can easily weigh larger amounts of food.

For the gram scale, an increment of 0.1 grams is normally good enough. Some scales increase by 0.01 grams, which is just fine, but probably a bit of overkill for most applications. The max weight is less important on the gram scale since most are above 100 grams.

Immersion Blenders

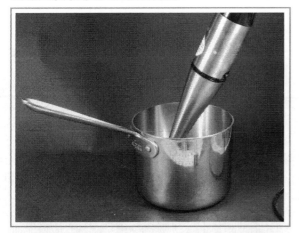

An immersion blender is one of those pieces of equipment that can seem silly and not very useful. However, once you own one you can't imagine cooking without it. In modernist cooking an immersion blender is needed to blend in many of the ingredients to ensure they are evenly mixed. If you already own a standing blender it can be used instead in many applications but the immersion blender is often more convenient.

In traditional cooking I use my immersion blender to puree sauces and soups directly in the pot, without having to get my blender dirty. I also use it to create purees from fresh vegetables and to quickly make vinaigrettes and mayonnaise.

Almost any immersion blender will work fine and they all are pretty similar in power.

Whisks

Whisks aren't used in any fancy ways but many ingredients need to be mixed together and whisks are a great way to do it. A set of decent whisks is very cheap and will come in handy in many situations.

HELPFUL ITEMS

There are many items that aren't required for all modernist cooking but have specific uses or make some aspects of cooking easier.

Weighing Dishes

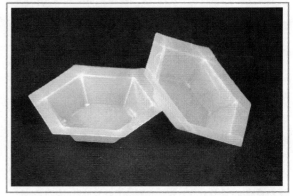

There are many types of dishes used in weighing, especially in weighing the small amounts of powder used in many recipes. They typically are anti-static and the powders don't stick to them as much as some other containers. They come in a few sizes and I recommend getting a few of each size. They will make measuring a lot easier and they usually are less than a dollar apiece.

If you don't want to get the dishes it can be useful to measure the powders on a piece of paper since they won't stick to it as much.

Hemispherical or Spherical Molds

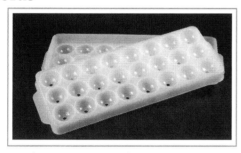

One of the interesting things about modernist cooking is the use of unusual shapes to present food. Hemispherical and spherical molds are an inexpensive way to shape your food. They work great with gels and make reverse spherification a breeze.

Plastic or Silicon Molds

Similar to the hemispherical molds, the silicon molds are a great way to create unusual shapes with your gels. They are inexpensive and come in a wide variety of shapes. You can also use many of the ice cube tray containers that are out there.

Acetate Sheets

Acetate sheets are commonly used to create films and thin gels, as well to line pans.

They are very useful if you are planning on making films, otherwise they are not needed.

Plastic Syringe and Tubing

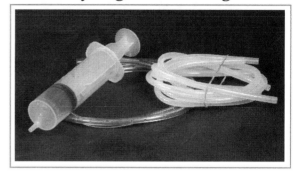

A plastic syringe has many uses in modernist cooking including making gel pearls and caviar. It can also be combined with food-grade plastic tubing to make gel noodles.

Spherification Tools

If you become interested in spherification there are several tools that can be very useful.

Rapid Caviar Maker

While using a plastic syringe to make caviar works well, it is a very slow process. If you commonly make caviar then it might be worth investing in a rapid caviar maker. It is a small box that drips liquid out, enabling you to make 50 to 100 caviar at once.

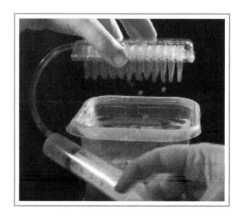

Caviar / Sphere Strainer

Getting the caviar and spheres out of the setting bath can be made easier with a proper spoon or strainer. Some traditional slotted spoons have holes that are too big. If that's the case then spending a few dollars on one designed for the smaller caviar can be a good idea.

Chinois

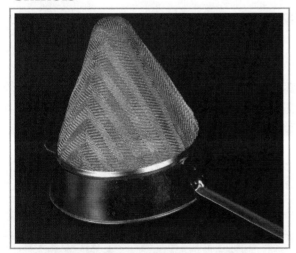

A chinois is a fine, metal strainer. It is great for removing pulp from purees and other liquids. You can use something like cheesecloth for many preparations but a chinois makes the process easier in many cases.

This equipment can be very useful both in modernist and traditional cooking. They are worth investing in if you find yourself commonly working with techniques that use them. We tried to focus on equipment that was easily accessible to home cooks and chefs on a budget, eschewing the very high-tech items like rotary evaporators.

Heat Resistant Whipping Siphon

This is one of my favorite toys to use. Its primary use is to create foams but it can also be used to carbonate liquids, fruits, and spheres.

A whipping siphon is basically a reusable whip cream container. You can pour some cream in it, add some powdered sugar, charge it with NO_2 and it will instantly dispense whipped cream.

It can be used in a similar manner with many fluid gels to create foams of different thicknesses. The heat resistant ones can also be used for hot foams and sauces.

If you are interested in making foams on a regular basis I highly recommend getting one.

Standing Blender

I love my immersion blender and use it with most preparations but sometimes I need the added power of a standing blender. It is much better at breaking down vegetables for purees and for crushing ice.

Sous Vide Machine

You can experiment with sous vide on the stove or in a beer cooler but if you are serious about using it on a regular basis it is worth getting some form of sous vide temperature controller. If you already have a crock pot or rice cooker you can get a controller that works with them and is around $200. Low end sous vide machines are a little more expensive and the high end runs around $800.

Juicer

Fruit and vegetable juices can be used with many modernist techniques to create gels, foams, and sauces. You can make juices with blenders and food processors but a juicer is more efficient and often easier to use.

Dehydrator

Dehydrators can be used for many things in modernist cooking such as setting foams and dehydrating gels. They also make great fruit or vegetable leathers and jerkies from any kind of meat.

Standing Mixer

For some foam preparations, such as marshmallows and meringues, a standing mixer with a whisk attachment is a necessity. It also has many uses in a traditional kitchen.

EVERYDAY MODERNIST COOKING

We are constantly adding recipes to our website as we continue to experiment with modernist cooking.
Maybe something there will inspire you.

You can find them at:
www.modernistcookingmadeeasy.com/info/modernist-recipes

Many of the recipes held up by the media as ideals of modernist cooking or molecular gastronomy are small, composed dishes with multiple components. This has given molecular gastronomy a reputation as being an elitist or "foodie only" way of cooking.

This section of the book is dedicated to showing you why this isn't true.

These dishes are things you can make on an everyday basis. In most cases they actually simplify the cooking process and often times speed it up as well.

Don't have time to reduce a sauce on the stove? No problem, add some xanthan gum.

Tired of burning a cream sauce when trying to thicken it? Try a little iota carrageenan.

In this section we try to focus on a few factors: convenience, flavor, and time saving. We also try to add a little bit of "wow" factor where we can.

THICKENING

Of all of the techniques used in modernist cooking, perhaps the most common one in everyday traditional cooking is thickening. All cooks have experience in thickening or thinning liquids. From turning chicken drippings into gravy, thickening a spaghetti sauce with tomato paste, reducing a sauce, or even adding more or less water to a pancake mix, thickening liquids is an integral part of cooking.

Because of how common thickening is, and how comfortable most cooks are with it, it is one of the easiest techniques to grasp for someone beginning with modernist cooking.

As with any cooking technique, modernist techniques aren't always better and can't replace old techniques. For instance, reducing a stock or a sauce has a concentration of flavors that is impossible to emulate with other thickening methods. However, knowing as many thickening techniques as possible allows you to select the best option in any cooking situation.

There are several advantages to using modernist ingredients.

Purity of Flavor

Using traditional thickening methods you are always modifying the flavor of the liquid. Whether reducing it through the addition of heat or thickening it by the addition of an ingredient such as flour or cream, the end result has a different flavor than the beginning liquid. In many cases this is preferred, but sometimes you want to taste the unadulterated flavors of the original liquid.

Using many of the ingredients outlined in this book allow you to thicken liquids with minimal modification to the flavor of the liquid.

Using Less Thickener
One of the ways this happens is due to the fact that you use so little of the thickener.

For example, most gravy recipes say to add 3% to 8% of flour to thicken it. Using xanthan gum you will add about 0.2% to 0.4%, or about 15 times less thickener.

This allows the flavor of the liquid to stand out much more.

No Heating
One way to thicken almost any liquid is to reduce it by heating it for an extended time.

However, sometimes you might not want to cook the food you are thickening, such as in a fruit puree. Using an ingredient that hydrates in low temperatures allows you to thicken these liquids without ever heating them.

Speed

Even if reducing a liquid would be the ideal way to thicken a sauce you are working on, occasionally you just don't have the time or patience to wait the 15 to 30 minutes for it to reduce. I especially run into this problem on work nights when dinner is already being served late.

Many modernist ingredients work very quickly and can be used as a great way to speed up the preparation of a meal.

ENTERTAINING

One of my favorite ways to use modernist cooking is creating appetizers, hors d'oeuvres, and amuse-bouches to use before parties or during larger dinners. I find it is a great way to showcase some interesting cooking without having to commit to cooking 12 different dishes.

Hors d'oeuvres

For parties I'll often make two or three plates of finger foods for people to snack on when they get there. I'll try to focus on a few dishes that can be made almost entirely ahead of time, that way I can spread the work over a few days, something that isn't always possible with more traditional appetizers.

Many of the typical modernist dishes are small plates that are part of a larger meal. One technique I like to use when I am having people over for dinner or a party is to use one or two of these dishes as hors d'oeuvres. The small size and fancy look is a great way to welcome guests and often times it gives them something to talk about.

"Wow" Dishes for Large Meals

For a larger dinner party I will try to plan one or two modernist dishes around a traditional dish that will be the center piece. For instance, I will plan on a traditional pot roast with mashed potatoes and vegetables but I'll first serve a deconstructed Caesar salad, or other modernist appetizer.

I will also put together an amuse-bouche to serve before or after the main course. This is especially easy if you focus on something that can be done ahead of time and held until dinner such as a frozen or cold foam, an infused drink, or a liquid sphere.

I've found that using modernist cooking for appetizers and amuse-bouches allows me to have fun, challenge my guests, and invite conversation while still providing a solid "meat and potatoes" centerpiece that even the less adventurous eaters will enjoy.

Desserts

Desserts are one more place I have fun experimenting with modernist techniques. It's also one of the places that my guests are most receptive to foams, fluid gels, and spheres.

If you don't bake, or just want to save time, you can even buy the main part of the dessert, like a cake or tarts. Then use a few modernist techniques to add garnishes like honey bubbles, a mango foam, or some hot chocolate spheres to really elevate the dish.

Drinks

Drinks are another place that many guests enjoy trying different things. They are often easy to make as well. You can take almost any fruit juice foam and use it with club soda and vodka or gin (or champagne!) for an easy mixed cocktail.

Spheres can be made ahead of time and used as garnishes instead of the ubiquitous canned maraschino cherries. And you can also gel the drinks in a variety of ways for a fancy version of Jell-O shots.

SAUCES AND VINAIGRETTES

There are several modernist ingredients that help make sauce making easier and more convenient, as well as allowing some unique control over the textures.

Common Sauce Ingredients

Xanthan Gum

Xanthan gum is great at adding thickness and mouthfeel to thin sauces. Typically, to thicken a sauce you have to reduce it on the stove. With a little xanthan gum you can get a similar effect while saving yourself the 15 to 30 minutes. Xanthan gum is also excellent at holding sauces together and making them cling to food better.

Agar Fluid Gels

Making a fluid gel from agar has a few steps, but they are all easy and can be done by spending 10 minutes at a time over a few days. You can gel most liquids with agar and then puree it into a nice, thick sauce.

Lecithin

Lecithin is great for helping to stabilize vinaigrettes, especially when used in conjunction with xanthan gum.

Benefits to Modernist Sauces

Convenience

Using modernist cooking techniques you can create emulsions and vinaigrettes ahead of time and they won't separate. They also make creating emulsions much easier with any ingredients.

Fat Reduction

Another benefit of modernist vinaigrettes and emulsions is that you can tailor the amount of oil you use. By adding thickeners to the vinaigrette you can greatly reduce the amount of oil you use. This can be good both for low-fat diets but is also great if you like to use high quality oils since it allows you to use less while getting the same flavor and body.

Body and Texture

The body and texture of your emulsions can also be changed to accommodate what you like. Want a thicker vinaigrette to flavor a steak? Add some more thickener. Prefer a runnier sauce but still want it to hold together, use less thickener but more emulsifier.

Controlling Flavor

Because the majority of the thickness is controlled by the thickeners used, you have better control over the flavors. You no longer have to add more oil to thicken it. Once the flavor you prefer has been obtained just add enough thickener to create the body you desire without altering the flavor.

SECTION TWO

MODERNIST COOKING TECHNIQUES

EMULSIFYING

Emulsifying is a very old cooking technique. Basically, it is when two liquids that don't mix become combined in a way that is stable. The most common household emulsion is probably a vinaigrette.

Since the two liquids are still separate they can fall out of suspension, causing the emulsion to "break". This is what happens when your bottle of vinaigrette has been sitting for awhile and the oil is all at the top with the vinegar at the bottom.

Each emulsion has two components, the "dispersed" liquid and the "continuous" liquid[3]. The dispersed liquid is distributed within the continuous liquid. For example, if a swimming pool full of people was an emulsion the people would be the "dispersed liquid" and the water would be the "continuous liquid".

The majority of culinary emulsions are water based. These emulsions can take one of two forms, either water-in-oil, where the water is dispersed in the oil, or oil-in-water, where the oil is dispersed in the water. Some common oil-in-water emulsions are mayonnaise, Hollandaise sauce, vinaigrettes, and milk. Butter is the most common example of a culinary water-in-oil emulsion.

STABILIZERS

Because emulsions are two different liquids that are in suspension, there is the tendency for them to separate and break apart. The way to counteract this is by adding something to strengthen the emulsion, which are called emulsifiers. These emulsifiers can work in a number of ways but they all make the emulsion stronger and less likely to break.

Several traditional emulsifiers are egg yolk (mayonnaise), mustard (vinaigrettes and sauces), and certain proteins (milk). Modernist cooking has introduced several new ones, many based on extracts from the traditional ones. For example, lecithin is the active emulsifier in egg yolks and can also be extracted from soy beans. Lecithin is also the emulsifier used to keep the cocoa butter and cocoa emulsified in chocolate bars.

Many of the newer emulsifiers are much stronger than the traditional ones. This means that a smaller amount has to be used to achieve the same result with even less of a change in flavor. Adding a teaspoon of mustard to your vinaigrette changes the flavor drastically (albeit often in a good way) while a gram of lecithin will preserve the initial flavors.

Another unique use of modernist emulsifiers is the ability to combine them in a way to reduce the amount of oil or fat needed. This helps create low-fat emulsions, including low-fat mayonnaise.

You can also create "cream" emulsions from any fat and liquid combination, instead of just milk fats. This allows many interesting applications such as a bacon "cream" or other flavored creams. As mentioned in *Modernist Cuisine*, you could also make a "cream" sauce used in kosher preparations since there would actually be no dairy in it.

EMULSION PROPERTIES

Droplet Size
The finer the droplet size, the more stable an emulsion usually is. Using mechanical tools like a blender can create very small droplets which allows the emulsion to last for much longer than just using a whisk.

Viscosity of Liquid
The higher the viscosity of the liquid, the more stable the emulsion will be. By adding thickeners such as xanthan gum you can increase the stability of the emulsion.

EMULSIFYING TOOLS

There are many different tools you can use make emulsions. The most common one is the whisk, which does an ok job for vinaigrettes that don't have to last as long.

A good option to the whisk is an immersion blender. It creates finer droplets in the emulsion which leads to greater stability. A standing blender or food processor also works very well.

At the high end of emulsion making are rotor-stator homogenizers, ultrasonic homogenizers, and the high-pressure homogenizer. These are all highly specialized tools that create incredible small droplets in emulsions.

VINAIGRETTES

Vinaigrettes are one of the most simple emulsions and most cooks are familiar with them. They are the combination of vinegar with oil, though in this book we refer to most mixtures of oil and liquid as a vinaigrette.

A basic vinaigrette is 1 part vinegar and 3 parts oil that is whisked or blended together. With modernist ingredients you can help stabilize the vinaigrette in a few ways.

Thickening the liquid will help keep the vinaigrette from breaking. This can be done with any of the thickeners but we typically use xanthan gum.

You can also strengthen the vinaigrette by adding an emulsifier. There are several different ones but lecithin or mono and diglycerides are our favorites.

The stabilization techniques can usually be used together for even stronger emulsions.

Vinaigrette Process
To make the strengthened vinaigrette I recommend creating a standard vinaigrette first and adjusting the seasoning as you like. Then you can blend in the stabilizers.

I prefer to use an immersion blender because it is the most convenient method for me, has very little clean up, and makes good emulsions.

Vinaigrette Ratios
For a typical vinaigrette, lecithin will be added as 0.5% to 1% of the liquid by weight. To help strengthen the emulsion you can add some xanthan gum at a 0.1% to 0.4% ratio, which will also slightly thicken it. You can also use mono and diglycerides at a 0.5% to 2.0% ratio.

BASIC STRENGTHENED VINAIGRETTE

The combination of lecithin and xanthan gum creates a vinaigrette that almost never breaks. This is a basic version of a red wine vinaigrette but you can use the lecithin and xanthan gum combination with almost any vinaigrette.

Makes 1 cup

Tools Needed
Lecithin
Xanthan gum
Immersion blender
A scale with small gram measurements

Ingredients
62 grams red wine vinegar, about ¼ cup
1 shallot, sliced
1 garlic clove, minced
Salt and pepper
165 grams olive oil, about ¾ cup
1.3 grams lecithin powder, 0.6%
0.45 grams xanthan gum, 0.2%

Combine the vinegar, shallot, garlic, salt, and pepper in a narrow bowl or mixing container that works well with your immersion blender. Let sit for 5 minutes. Blend in the olive oil with an immersion blender or whisk attachment.

Taste the vinaigrette for seasoning and adjust the olive oil and vinegar to control the acidity.

Once the vinaigrette tastes balanced to you add the xanthan gum and lecithin then blend well to combine. Taste the vinaigrette and make sure the mouthfeel and thickness is what you prefer. Add more xanthan gum or liquid to adjust the thickness.

It is now ready to be served.

Basic Thickened Herb Vinaigrette

Another way to easily emulsify a vinaigrette is to thicken it. The thicker liquid helps to hold its shape more and trap the oil inside. An added benefit of a thickened vinaigrette is that it more easily clings to and coats the food.

You can easily tweak this recipe to be thicker or thinner and to change the flavors how you like.

I really like this vinaigrette on fish or chicken, although it is also great on salad.

Makes 1 cup

Tools Needed
Xanthan gum
Immersion blender
A scale with small gram measurements

Ingredients
62 grams white wine vinegar, about ¼ cup
1 shallot, sliced
Salt and pepper
165 grams olive oil, about ¾ cup
0.45 grams xanthan gum, 0.2%
½ cup fresh basil, chopped
½ cup fresh parsley, chopped

Combine the vinegar, shallot, salt, and pepper in a narrow bowl or mixing container that works well with your immersion blender. Let sit for 5 minutes. Blend in the olive oil with an immersion blender.

Taste the vinaigrette for seasoning and adjust the olive oil and vinegar to control the acidity.

Once the vinaigrette tastes balanced to you add the xanthan gum and blend well to combine. Taste the vinaigrette and make sure the mouthfeel and thickness is what you prefer. Add more xanthan gum or liquid to adjust the thickness.

Once the thickness is what you want stir in the basil and parsley.

The vinaigrette can now be served at any time or can be held for several hours. If holding for longer than a few hours you can refrigerate for a day or two before it breaks.

Tomatillo Sauce

Tomatillos have a natural acidity in them that can work really well in a vinaigrette-like sauce. The sauce comes together very quickly and can be tweaked in many directions. In this recipe I flavor the sauce with some honey, garlic, and cilantro but you could also add serrano peppers for a spicy sauce, or avocado and lime for a slant on guacamole. This sauce is great on flank steak or a white fish like cod. It can even be used as a salad dressing.

Makes about 1 cup

Tools Needed
Xanthan gum
Standing blender
A scale with small gram measurements

Ingredients
150 grams tomatillos, dehusked, washed, and
    stem removed
42 grams honey, about 2 tablespoons
2-4 cloves garlic, roughly chopped
Several cilantro springs, roughly chopped
55 grams olive oil, about ¼ cup
Salt and pepper
0.25-0.5 grams xanthan gum, 0.1-0.2%

Place the tomatillos, honey, garlic, and cilantro in a blender. Puree until smooth.

Drizzle in the olive oil while the blender is running. Salt and pepper to taste and taste to ensure the acidity and sweetness is balanced.

Once the sauce has the flavor you want, add the xanthan gum, starting at the lower end, and puree to mix. Taste the vinaigrette and make sure the mouthfeel and thickness is what you prefer. Add more xanthan gum or water to adjust the thickness as needed.

The tomatillo sauce can be served at any time or can be held for several hours. If holding for longer than a few hours you can refrigerate for a day or two before it separates. You can give it a quick blend with a blender before serving if it has separated.

CHIPOTLE VINAIGRETTE

This is a nice and spicy vinaigrette that can be used on taco salad or any salad you want to give a kick to. You can also add a little more xanthan gum and use it as a sauce on fish, chicken, or steak.

This recipe makes about ¾ cup.

Tools Needed
Lecithin
Xanthan gum
Immersion blender
A scale with small gram measurements

Ingredients
50 grams lime juice, preferably fresh
1 chipotle in adobo sauce
1 garlic cloves, roughly chopped
Salt and pepper
90 grams olive oil
Several cilantro sprigs
0.8 grams lecithin powder, 0.6%
0.2 grams xanthan gum, 0.2%

Combine the lime juice, chipotle pepper, garlic, salt, and pepper in a narrow bowl or mixing container that works well with your immersion blender. Blend in the olive oil with an immersion blender or whisk attachment.

Taste the vinaigrette for seasoning and adjust the olive oil and lime juice to control the acidity.

Once the vinaigrette tastes balanced to you add the xanthan gum and lecithin then blend well to combine. Taste the vinaigrette and make sure the mouthfeel and thickness is what you prefer. Add more xanthan gum or liquid to adjust the thickness.

Add the cilantro and blend it briefly with the immersion blender. It is now ready to be served.

SPRING SALSA

This spring salsa is very simple to make and really adds some lightness and flavor to a dish. It's great in late spring when the cherry tomatoes are just starting to ripen. It also goes well with steak, chicken or turkey breasts.

We use a little xanthan gum in the dressing for the salsa to hold it together and cling to the vegetable chunks better.

Tools Needed
Xanthan gum
Immersion blender
A scale with small gram measurements

Ingredients
For the Dressing
15 grams water, about 1 tablespoon
30 grams white wine vinegar, about 2
    tablespoons
55 grams olive oil, about ¼ cup
Salt and pepper
0.15 grams xanthan gum, 0.15%

For the Salsa
1 cup cherry tomatoes, halved
5 radishes, diced
1 cup corn kernels, cooked
¼ red onion, diced
¼ cup chopped fresh basil

Combine the water, white wine vinegar, olive oil, salt, and pepper in a narrow bowl or mixing container that works well with your immersion blender. Blend well with an immersion blender.

Taste the dressing for seasoning and adjust the olive oil and vinegar to control the acidity.

Once the dressing tastes balanced, add the xanthan gum and blend well to combine.

Mix all of the salsa ingredients in a bowl and top with the dressing.

Raspberry Salad

This is a nice and bright summer salad. It's great when served with a seared white fish like cod or sea bass but it can even hold up next to a grilled steak.

Tools Needed

Xanthan gum
Immersion blender
A scale with small gram measurements

Ingredients

For the Dressing
30 grams raspberry or raspberry champagne
    vinegar, about 2 tablespoons
15 grams orange juice, about 1 tablespoon
1 shallot, diced
2 grams honey, about 2 tablespoons
75 grams olive oil, about 5 tablespoons
Salt and pepper
0.3 grams xanthan gum, 0.3%

For the Salad
Mixed baby greens or the lettuce of your choice
½ yellow or red bell pepper, diced
10 cherry tomatoes, halved
¼ cup fresh raspberries or mixed berries
2 radishes, sliced
2 tablespoons sunflower seeds

Combine all the dressing ingredients except for the xanthan gum in a narrow bowl or mixing container that works well with your immersion blender. Blend well with an immersion blender.

Taste the dressing for seasoning and adjust the olive oil and vinegar to control the acidity.

Once the dressing tastes balanced, add the xanthan gum and blend well to combine.

Assemble the salad by placing the lettuce on plates. Top with the pepper, tomatoes, raspberries, and radishes. Drizzle the vinaigrette on the salad and top with the sunflower seeds. Lightly sprinkle the salad with salt and pepper and serve.

FENNEL COLESLAW

I like the flavor of fennel in coleslaw, it adds a nice licorice taste that elevates the dish. The snow peas add great bursts of sweetness that complement the citrus vinaigrette. The xanthan gum and lecithin here help bind the vinaigrette as well as coat the slaw without all running to the bottom of the bowl.

Tools Needed
Xanthan gum
Lecithin
Immersion blender
Strainer
A scale with small gram measurements

Ingredients
For the Vinaigrette
73 grams orange juice, preferably fresh, about 5 tablespoons
15 grams white wine vinegar, about 1 tablespoon
13 grams olive oil , about 3 tablespoons
Salt and pepper
0.6 grams lecithin powder, 0.6%
0.2 grams xanthan gum, 0.2%

For the Slaw
1 small fennel bulb, trimmed, cored, and shredded
5 large carrots, peeled and shredded
1 cup snow pea pods, cut into long strips
¼ red onion, minced
½ cup fresh cilantro, chopped
⅓ cup sliced almonds, toasted

First make the dressing. Combine the orange juice, vinegar, olive oil, salt, and pepper in a narrow bowl or mixing container that works well with your immersion blender. Blend well with an immersion blender.

Taste the dressing for seasoning and adjust the olive oil and vinegar to control the acidity.

Once the dressing tastes balanced, add the xanthan gum and lecithin then blend well to combine.

Mix all of the slaw ingredients except for the almonds in a bowl and toss well with the dressing.

Sprinkle the pecans on top and serve.

FOAMS

We have a fan page on Facebook. You can follow us there for updated recipes, tips, and equipment reviews.

You can find it at:
www.facebook.com/ModernistCookingMadeEasy

Foams are one of the techniques most associated with modernist cooking, and with good reason. They are easy to make, very versatile, and fun to use and eat. Foams have been around traditional cooking for a very long time and include whipped cream, head on beer, and even bread dough.

At the most basic level, foams are a structure that traps air in bubbles. Foams are similar in this way to an emulsion, which is when a liquid traps fat in a structure, or fat traps liquids in a structure.

The structure can be made from a variety of things such as proteins, water, or fat. The texture of the foam is determined by the size of the bubbles and how much liquid is in the foam. Some foams are considered "set" foams, which means the structure has been solidified, such as when baking bread dough or a soufflé.

SPECTRUMS OF FOAMS

Whether they are called bubbles, airs, meringues, espumas, puffs, or froths, all foams share certain characteristics. Similar to gels, these characteristics lie on a spectrum.

Fine vs Coarse

The texture of a foam ranges from fine to coarse and refers to the size and uniformness of the bubbles.

A foam where the bubbles are smaller and very uniform is considered fine. Whipped cream is an example of a fine foam.

A foam with larger and less uniform bubbles are considered coarse. Some examples of coarse foams are latte froth, airs, and the head on light beer.

Dry vs Wet

The wetness of a foam refers to the amount of liquid that is in the structure of the bubbles. Usually, the coarser a foam is, the dryer it is.

Dry foams are mainly air and can be very light. The bubbles are typically larger and their flavor is diluted due to the lack of liquid. Most very dry foams are referred to as "airs".

Wet foams have much more liquid in their structure. They can range from light to dense foams. They are usually fine foams, rather than coarse foams. Most foams you know are wet foams such as whipped cream and milkshake froth.

Airy vs Dense

Foams can range from very light, such as airs, to very dense, mousse-like foams similar to whipped cream. The density depends on the texture and wetness of a foam. The finer the bubbles are and the wetter the foam is the denser it becomes.

TYPES OF FOAMS

There are different names for types of foams. Some of these are interchangeable and none of the definitions are set in stone.

To understand what people are talking about regarding foams, it's important that you learn the characteristics associated with the following names.

Airs

Typically a dry, coarse foam that is mainly made up of air. Strongly flavored liquids should be used in airs because they have such little liquid.

Dense Foams

Dense foams refer to thicker, fine, wet foams. They usually have smaller bubbles. Whip cream is a good example of a dense foam.

Light Foams

Light foams lie somewhere in between airs and dense foams. They are finer and wetter than airs but not as thick as dense foams.

Bubbles

Like airs, bubbles are coarse foams but they tend to have more liquid in them than airs do and are made up of larger bubbles. They usually resemble common bubbles like those created by soap or shampoo.

Froths

Froths are usually wet but coarse foams. They are named after the froth that is often on the top of a milkshake or latte.

Set Foams

Set foams are foams that have had their structure solidified. This is often done through heating or dehydrating. A loaf of bread and a baked soufflé are examples.

Espumas

"Espuma" is the Spanish word for foam and they are usually dense foams. They are always created by a whipping siphon and usually served hot.

Meringues and Puffs

Meringues and puffs are lighter foams that are often baked or dehydrated to set their structure.

STABILIZING FOAMS

In order for a foam to last more than a few seconds it needs to be stabilized. There are many ways to stabilize a foam, often by thickening or gelling the liquid.

For best foaming action be sure to pick liquids that are thin and watery and do not contain many particles. If you want to make a foam from a thicker sauce you can try watering it down until it becomes thinner and running it through a chinois if there are larger particles in it.

Thickened Liquid Foams

One of the simplest ways to create a foam is to combine a liquid with a thickening ingredient, such as xanthan gum. Then you introduce air to it, usually through whipping, blending, or using a whipping siphon. This usually results in a coarse, wet foam that is on the lighter side.

Xanthan gum is usually added in a 0.2% to 0.8% ratio, depending on the density of foam desired.

Stabilized Foams

Similar to thickened liquid foams, stabilized foams combine a stabilizer such as lecithin or Versawhip with the liquid. The resulting foam tends to be a little finer than thickened liquid foams. These can usually be made with most of the foaming equipment listed in this chapter.

Using traditional stabilizing agents like egg white, cream, and sugar are also effective. Many of the things in those ingredients that stabilize the foam have been isolated and are sold as separate ingredients, such as lecithin. These are also incorporated into other modernist ingredients such as Versawhip.

A ratio of 0.5% to 1.0% is commonly used for Versawhip. Lecithin is used at a 0.25% to 1.0% ratio. Xanthan gum can also be added for thickening at 0.1% to 0.5%.

Fluid Gel Foams

An effective way to create thicker foams is by using gels and fluid gels. You first turn the liquid you want to foam into a gel. Often times agar, carrageenan, gelatin, or methylcellulose are used to create the gel, or fluid gel.

Depending on the ingredient, the gel can be whipped or put in a whipping siphon to create a foam. These foams have a range of textures and densities depending on the fluid gel used.

Agar fluid gels are usually made with a 0.25% to 1.0% ratio. Gelatin is used with a 0.4% to 1.7%. Xanthan gum can also be added to the above ingredients to thicken the foam, typically in a 0.1% to 0.4% ratio.

FOAMING EQUIPMENT

There are many tools you can use to create foams and each one results in a slightly different texture. The purpose of all the tools is to introduce air into the liquid you are foaming. For tools such as whisks and immersion blenders you want to make sure part of the tool is out of the liquid so it will carry air into the foam.

Whisks, Manual and Electric

Whisks are a great way to create dense foams as well as some lighter foams. Manual whisks can get the job done but using an electric whisk attachment greatly speeds up the process and tends to form finer foams. The whisk attachment can be on an immersion blender or a standing mixer.

Standing or Hand Held Mixer

Mixers without a whisk attachment can also be used. They can create lighter foams very efficiently.

Milk Frother

A milk frother is an inexpensive tool that is used to create foam for cappuccinos or lattes. When it used with modernist ingredients it can create similar foams from other liquids. Aerolatte brand frothers are usually under $20.

Immersion Blender

Immersion blenders are good at creating airs and other light foams. Ensuring part of the blade is out of the liquid is critical. A traditional standing blender will not work well for foaming because the blades are completely submerged.

Whipping Siphon

The whipping siphon is an awesome tool for making foams of all kinds. It is a container you fill with liquid and then pressurize with NO_2 or occasionally CO_2. They are very effective at creating foams and also help in the storage of liquids you will be foaming over time.

Aquarium Bubbler

An aquarium bubbler is one of the more unusual ways to create foams. It works well for creating large bubbles, similar to soap bubbles. Tetra Whisper brand pumps can typically be found for under $10.

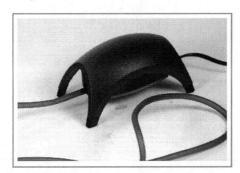

LIGHT FOAMS

Light foams can be airy, coarse foams or wet, fine foams. They are also the easiest to make without additional kitchen equipment like a whipping siphon or standing mixer.

You can make light foams in a few different ways but either an immersion blender or electric whisk works well, as do milk frothers or aquarium bubblers for specific types of foams.

To make a light foam you combine the liquid you want to foam with the foaming agent. For light foams the foaming agent is typically lecithin, sometimes with some xanthan gum added to create wetter froths.

Once the foaming agent has been incorporated you add air to the liquid through whipping or blending. If you are using an immersion blender you want to keep half of the blade out of the liquid so the maximum amount of air will be introduced.

Depending on the liquid and foaming agents used, the light foam will last for 30 to 60 minutes. However, it will lose body the longer it sits.

You can spoon the light foam directly onto a dish or freeze it for a cold, ethereal treat.

Light Foam Ratios

At the dryer end of the spectrum, most airs use 0.25% to 1.0% lecithin, though the specific amount isn't as important as in many other techniques.

For wetter foams, xanthan gum can be added at 0.1% to 0.4%. The more xanthan gum added, the wetter the foam will tend to be.

For bubbles, resembling soap bubbles, a typical ratio is 0.1% to 0.4% xanthan gum and 0.2% to 2.0% Versawhip or egg white powder.

Soy Air

Airs are typically dry, coarse foams that are mainly made up of air. Strongly flavored liquids should be used in airs because they have such little liquid. Here we used soy sauce which adds a salty, umami flavor to dishes. This recipe can be used with most liquids to create airs.

This soy air is a great garnish for Asian flavored tuna or pork.

Tools Needed
Lecithin
Immersion blender
Flat bottomed, wide container
A scale with small gram measurements

Ingredients
125 grams water
125 grams soy sauce
8 grams sugar
1 gram lecithin, 0.4%

Combine the water, soy sauce, and sugar in a sauce pan. Bring to a simmer while whisking occasionally to break up any lumps. Remove from the heat and blend in the lecithin with an immersion blender.

Pour it into a wide, flat bottomed, container. You can set the soy sauce mixture aside like this for several hours.

When ready to serve, blend the soy sauce mixture using an immersion blender until a nice head of foam develops. While blending try to keep the immersion blender halfway out of the liquid so it will incorporate as much air as possible.

Let the soy foam sit for 1 minute to stabilize and then spoon it out onto your dish.

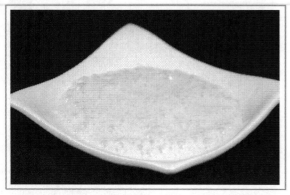

This orange froth is a good way to add a different texture to a dish, as well as an interesting visual component. It is wetter than an air but still very light.

It can be used on tropical salads or as a sauce for white fish. It is also good on desserts or fruit salads. If you enjoy mimosas this can be a unique way to add the fruit juice to it as well. It can also be used as an amuse bouche between courses, especially if you use a whipping siphon to foam it.

Tools Needed
Lecithin
Xanthan gum
Immersion blender
Flat bottomed, wide container
A scale with small gram measurements

Ingredients
250 grams orange juice, preferably fresh
1.8 grams lecithin, .75%
0.75 grams xanthan gum, 0.3%

Strain the orange juice if it has a lot of pulp since it will inhibit the formation of bubbles.

Place the orange juice in a container that works well with your immersion blender. Sprinkle in the lecithin and xanthan gum and blend to combine well. Pour into a wide, flat bottomed container. You can set the mixture aside like this for several hours.

When ready to serve, blend the orange juice mixture using an immersion blender until a nice head of foam develops. Try to keep the immersion blender halfway out of the liquid so it will incorporate as much air as possible.

Let the orange froth sit for 1 minute to stabilize and then spoon it out onto your dish.

These bubbles are large and visually interesting. They also carry a surprising amount of flavor. I originally wanted to make these to use with a peanut butter panna cotta for a take on a PB&J but it can be used on many different dishes. You can also substitute the grape juice for just about any other fruit or vegetable juice.

Combine the grape juice with the Versawhip in a narrow, deep container and blend with the immersion blender to combine. Add the xanthan gum and blend until it is evenly distributed. You can set the mixture aside like this for several hours.

When ready to serve, connect a clean piece of plastic hosing to the aquarium pump and place the other end in the mixture. Turn on the pump and let it create bubbles until there are enough for you to use.

Let the bubbles sit for 1 minute to stabilize and then spoon them out onto your dish.

Tools Needed
Versawhip
Xanthan gum
Immersion blender
Aquarium pump with plastic hose
A scale with small gram measurements

Ingredients
400 grams grape juice
2.0 grams Versawhip, 0.5%
1.0 grams xanthan gum, 0.25%

An easy way to create flavorful light foams is to go through your teas and see what you have on hand. This uses the Celestial Seasonings' Raspberry Zinger tea to create a light and tasty raspberry foam.

It is great on desserts or as a base for fish seasoned with a tropical flair.

The recipe calls to use a whipping siphon but if you don't have one you can aerate it using almost any of the other foaming equipment. The foam will not be the exact same but it will still work well.

Tools Needed
Xanthan gum
Immersion blender
Whipping siphon
A scale with small gram measurements

Ingredients
400 grams water
2-3 Raspberry Zinger tea packets
3.2 grams xanthan gum, 0.8%

Bring the water to a boil. Add the tea and let steep for 5 to 10 minutes. Add the xanthan gum and blend with the immersion blender until it is evenly distributed.

If you do not have a heat resistant whipping siphon then let the tea mixture cool to room temperature. Pour the tea mixture into a whipping siphon and charge as recommended.

It can be held like this until you are ready to use it, several hours or over night in the refrigerator.

If you are serving it cold, refrigerate it. If you are serving it hot, and you have a heat resistant whipping siphon, you can place it in a water bath to heat it.

To serve, simply turn the whipping siphon upside down and dispense the foam.

FLUID GEL FOAMS

Fluid gel foams are denser and much finer than light foams and airs. They are usually very wet and thick, with a texture similar to shaving cream. Fluid gel foams are best made with a whipping siphon.

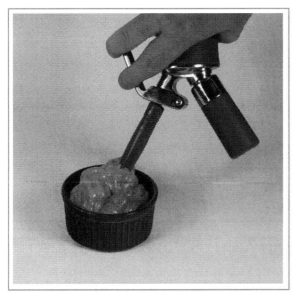

To make a fluid gel foam, you first create a fluid gel[4]. Some good gelling agents are agar, carrageenan, gelatin, or methylcellulose. Once you have the fluid gel, place it in a whipping siphon and charge it. For some gels, like gelatin gels, you need to refrigerate it for a few hours so it can set. Once it's set you can dispense the foam.

Fluid Gel Foam Ratios

In general, the thicker the fluid gel is, the thicker the resulting foam will be. For a detailed look at the various gelling agents you can see their chapter later in the book. Some general guidelines are:

Agar - 0.25% to 1.0%
Carrageenan: Iota - 0.2% to 1.0%
Gelatin - 0.4% to 1.7%
Methylcellulose - 1.0% to 3.0%

You can also add xanthan gum, typically at a 0.1 to 0.4% ratio, to change the texture of the foam. Other thickeners work as well.

Different stabilizers also can change the textures of the foams and are often combined with the gelling agent. This includes egg white, Versawhip, lecithin and many others.

BLACKCURRANT FOAM

Blackcurrant is an usual berry in the United States but is much more common in Europe. This foam is on the thicker side and is full of flavor. It can be used on desserts to add some sweet and tart flavor or as a sauce with fish. You can also make a twist on Kir, a classic French cocktail, by topping some white wine with the foam.

Tools Needed
Gelatin
Whipping siphon
A scale with small gram measurements

Ingredients
400 grams blackcurrant juice
Sugar or honey, optional
2 gelatin sheets or ½ packet, 0.9%

Taste the blackcurrant juice and add sugar or honey to sweeten it if needed.

Pour 75 to 100 grams of blackcurrant juice into a pot with the gelatin. Let the gelatin bloom for 5 to 10 minutes.

Once the gelatin has bloomed heat the pot over medium to medium-high heat while stirring until the gelatin has dissolved and is evenly dispersed. Stir in the remaining blackcurrant juice.

Pour the blackcurrant mixture into a whipping siphon and charge with nitrous oxide according to the manufacturer's directions. Refrigerate the whipping siphon until the gelatin sets, typically 2 to 3 hours.

Dispense the foam when you are ready to serve your dishes.

CHOCOLATE FOAM

This thick chocolate foam is a great way to top ice cream or a brownie. It can even be served by itself, dusted with some cinnamon and powdered sugar. It has to be served below room temperature but it is still a versatile sauce.

I just call for general hot chocolate in the recipe but the higher quality the hot chocolate you use the better. For this recipe I prefer a much darker hot chocolate than I would usually drink, that way the foam has a deeper chocolate flavor. I also like it on the sweeter side.

Tools Needed
Gelatin
Whipping siphon
A scale with small gram measurements

Ingredients
500 grams hot chocolate, cold
4 gelatin sheets or 1 packet, 1.4%

Place the cold hot chocolate in a pot with the gelatin. Let the gelatin bloom for 5 to 10 minutes.

Once the gelatin has bloomed heat the pot over medium to medium-high heat while stirring until the gelatin has dissolved and is evenly dispersed.

Pour the hot chocolate mixture into a whipping siphon and charge with nitrous oxide according to the manufacturer's directions. Refrigerate the whipping siphon until the gelatin sets, typically 2 to 3 hours.

Dispense the foam when you are ready to serve your dishes.

A common pairing is coffee and steak. This coffee foam takes that pairing and elevates it, turning the coffee into a thick foam that is used as a sauce for the steak.

You can also use this foam on a variety of desserts, especially ice cream or gelato. For desserts, you will most likely want to add a good amount of cream and sugar. If you are using it on a cold dessert, you may want to skip the step at the end where you heat the siphon.

Tools Needed
Agar
Xanthan gum
Standing or immersion blender
Whipping siphon
A scale with small gram measurements

Ingredients
500 grams coffee
5.0 grams agar, 1.0%
0.5 grams xanthan gum, 0.1%

Blend the coffee, agar, and xanthan gum together with the immersion blender or standing blender. Add to a pot. Bring to a boil and let simmer for 3 to 5 minutes so the agar can hydrate. Pour into a container and let it completely set.

Once it is set, cube the gel and puree with a blender until smooth. Add some water if you need to thin it, or some more xanthan gum to thicken it. It should be just barely pourable.

Pour the fluid gel into your whipping siphon and charge. Heat the whipper in hot water until it is warm, I tend to use water between 55°C / 131°F to 60.5°C / 141°F because that is what my sous vide machine is running at but any water below 80°C / 175°F should be fine.

Once the foam has come up to temperature you can dispense it onto your dishes.

WHIPPED FOAMS

Whipped foams are dense, wet foams such as whipped cream or meringues. Whipped foams are best made with a whipping siphon or a standing mixer with a whisk attachment. Some can be made with an electric hand mixer or a hand whisk but many of the thicker foams are just too dense for these tools.

Whipped foams are created by dispersing a stabilizer into a liquid and then whipping it until peaks are formed. The stabilizer will help the foam stay together. In whipped cream the stabilizer is traditionally the fat in the cream and for meringues it is the proteins in the egg white.

For modernist foams you can also use methylcellulose, Versawhip, or other stabilizers.

After you have created the whipped foam you have a few options on how to use it. You can serve it directly, like whipped cream on pie. You can also dehydrate the foam to create a meringue. Some foams can also be frozen. When serving it directly you can either spoon it out or use a pastry bag or a ziploc bag with the corner cut off.

Whipped Foam Ratios

The amount of stabilizer you use depends on how stiff you want the foams, as well as the specific stabilizer you are using.

In general you use Methocel F50 at a 1.0% to 2.0% with 0.1% to 0.3% xanthan gum. For Versawhip, a 0.5% to 2.0% ratio is ideal with 0.1% to 0.2% xanthan gum.

Whipped cream is very easy to make with a whipping siphon. For this recipe I added some key lime juice to help bring some acidity and brightness to the resulting whipped cream. You could also add other flavors such as triple sec or amaretto, strawberry syrup, vanilla extract, mint extract, or anything else you would like to flavor the cream with.

Tools Needed
Whipping Siphon

Ingredients
Note: All measurements are for a 1 pint whipping siphon, scale them up or down depending on the size of siphon you have.
1 pint heavy cream or whipping cream (2 cups)
2 tablespoons powdered / confectioners sugar
2-3 tablespoons fresh key lime juice

Combine all the ingredients in a bowl and mix well. Pour the mixture into the whipping siphon and seal. Charge with a N_2O cartridge.

The whipped cream is now ready to serve but you can refrigerate the whipped cream siphon at this point until you are ready to use it.

To serve, shake the siphon several times. Turn the siphon upside down and dispense directly onto the dish.

MANGO FOAM

Versawhip and xanthan gum combine to make light foams that are a great way to add texture to dishes. It's a great topping for desserts and ice creams or can even be eaten as an amuse bouche between dishes.

You can also create stiffer foams by whipping it until firm peaks form, instead of the soft peaks.

Tools Needed

Versawhip 600
Xanthan gum
Standing or immersion blender
Standing mixer with whisk attachment
A scale with small gram measurements

Ingredients

300 grams mango juice
3.75 grams Versawhip 600, 1.25%
0.45 grams xanthan gum, 0.15%

Blend the juice, Versawhip, and xanthan gum to combine well.

Pour the juice mixture into the bowl of a stand mixer fitted with a whisk attachment. Whisk until soft peaks form, 3 to 10 minutes.

The foam is then ready to be used. It can also be stored in the refrigerator for several days and re-whipped as needed.

A great way to make meringues is to use flavored teas. Stash makes a good peach-ginger tea that we use in this recipe to flavor the meringues.

When using teas I will typically use one and a half to two times as much tea as usual. This helps to up the flavor to counteract the dilution due to all the added air during the whipping process.

You can use these meringues as components on dessert plates or even as a side garnish for more savory foods. They are also great just eaten as snacks.

In this recipe I give instructions for dehydrating the foam but you can also serve it fresh if you prefer.

Tools Needed
Methocel F50
Xanthan gum
Standing blender
Standing mixer with whisk attachment
Dehydrator or oven
Pastry bag or ziploc bag
A scale with small gram measurements

Ingredients
200 grams brewed peach-ginger tea
2 grams Methocel F50, 1.0%
0.3 grams xanthan gum, 0.15%

Place the tea in a standing blender. Turn the blender on to a speed where a vortex forms. Sprinkle the Methocel F50 and xanthan gum into the vortex and continue to blend for 30 to 60 seconds to ensure even dispersion. Place the tea in the refrigerator for several hours to hydrate.

Once fully hydrated, remove the tea from the refrigerator and whip it with the standing mixer with the whisk attachment until peaks form, about 5 to 10 minutes.

Spoon the foam into a pastry bag or a ziploc bag with the corner cut off.

Using a Dehydrator
Line a dehydrator tray with a silicone mat or parchment paper. Pipe small mounds onto the tray. Dehydrate for 3 to 5 hours, until it turns crispy and is fully dehydrated.

Using an Oven
Line a sheet pan or cookie sheet with a silicone mat or parchment paper. Pipe small mounds onto the tray. Set the oven to low, place the meringues into it, and leave the door slightly ajar. Let the meringues dehydrate for 2 to 6 hours, until they turn crispy and are fully dehydrated.

GELLING

We are constantly adding recipes to our website as we continue
to experiment with modernist cooking.
Maybe something there will inspire you.

You can find them at:
www.modernistcookingmadeeasy.com/info/modernist-recipes

Gelling is a wide ranging and very important technique in traditional and modern cooking. It encapsulates everything from the old to the new, from custards to edible gel sheets to spherification. There are many different ingredients that cause gelling including eggs, starches like flour, and hydrocolloids like agar and xanthan gum.

How Gelling Works

Gelling is a very interesting process. There are a few different ways gelling happens but most of them result in some kind of solid structure that traps liquid in it. The structure is often made of proteins and gives form and body to the gel.

To achieve this structure we have to add gelling agents to the liquid we want to gel. There are many traditional gelling ingredients most cooks are familiar with. Gelatin is often used in desserts as well as naturally providing body in stocks. Cooked eggs become gels. Even the proteins in flour form a network for doughs.

Now, there are a variety of new gelling agents, many of which are called hydrocolloids, that give us a lot more control over the types of gels we create.

Gel Spectrums

One of the biggest hurdles I had when learning about modernist cooking was understand the vocabulary for the different properties of gels. Many of the properties can be expressed by a spectrum so I've tried to explain them that way.

Different ingredients, and different concentrations of ingredients, can move the gel along these spectrums. For instance, agar

gels are brittle and iota carrageenan forms elastic gels. But if you combine agar with locust bean gum the gel begins to become more elastic.

Brittle vs Elastic

All gels fall somewhere on the brittle vs elastic spectrum. On the brittle side, gels easily fall apart with pressure, are grainy, and crumble easily.

Conversely, elastic gels are more flexible, jiggly, and chewy. Gummy bears are a good example of an elastic gel.

Soft vs Firm

All gels also lie somewhere on the soft vs firm spectrum. Soft gels give under pressure and have a much more tender texture. Firm gels resist pressure and hold their shape better.

The softness or firmness of most gels can be controlled by the amount of gelling agent used. Adding a higher percent of a gelling agent results in a firmer gel. Custards and

Jell-O are a good example of soft gels and gummy bears are a firm gel.

Sticky vs Clean

The final spectrum that gels are on is sticky vs clean. Sticky gels tend to adhere to surfaces, and your mouth, similar to taffy or carmel. Clean gels do not stick to other substances, similar to Jell-O.

OTHER PROPERTIES OF GELS

There are many other properties that a gel can have. Depending on how you are planning to use a gel they may or may not be important for any given preparation.

Setting Temperature

The setting temperature of a gel is the temperature below which the gel will form[5]. For instance, gelatin has to be refrigerated before it sets while agar will set once it drops below 45°C / 113°F.

Melting Temperature

The melting temperature of a gel is the temperature above which it will unset and become a liquid again. For example, gelatin tends to melt at a hot picnic while agar can be heated up to 80°C / 175°F before it begins to melt.

Not all gels have a melting temperature, such as thermo-irreversible gels, and will never melt.

Syneresis

Syneresis is the leaking out, or weeping, of liquids from a gel. Sometimes this is the desired result such as when using a gel to clarify a liquid. However, most of the time syneresis is unwanted. Different gels have different levels of syneresis and many times

you can prevent it by combining one or more ingredients. Locust bean gum is typically good at preventing syneresis with other gelling agents.

Clarity

The clarity of a gel is simply how clear it is. Gels can range from transparent to opaque. This is affected by the gelling ingredients and also the opacity of the liquid that makes up the gel.

Flavor Release

How well a gel will release the flavors of the liquid it is made of is referred to as its flavor release. Some gelling agents like gelatin have good flavor release while others tend to lock up the flavors more.

Freeze-Thaw Stability

If a gel can be frozen and then thawed without losing its structure it is considered freeze-thaw stable. This is a very important consideration if the gel is a part of foods made to be frozen and thawed.

Hysteresis

This is a very interesting property of gels. It basically means that the setting and melting temperatures are not the same. The higher the hysteresis, the larger the distance between the temperatures. For instance, water sets and melts at 0°C / 32°F, so if it's below 0°C / 32°F it will freeze, and if it's above 0°C / 32°F then it will melt.

Agar, on the other hand, has a setting temperature around 40°C / 104°F and a melting temperature of 85°C / 185°F. This means if agar is a solid, then it will remain a solid until heated above 80°C / 176°F. Then as it cools, it will remain a liquid until it goes below 40°C / 104°F. The result is between 40°C / 104°F and 80°C / 176°F an agar gel can be either a solid or a liquid.

Particle Suspending

As discussed early, a gel is typically a solid structure that traps liquid. However, this structure can also trap other solid particles in it, suspending them. This is very useful for holding herbs in a vinaigrette or tomato chunks in a puree.

Thermoreversibility

If a gel can get set and then melt, like Jell-O melting on a warm day, then it is considered thermoreversible. If the gel cannot be unset, like a soufflé, then it is considered thermo-irreversible. Most thermoreversible gels can be set and unset many times without a loss in gelling strength.

Shear Thinning or Thixotropy[6]

Both of these terms refer to the ability to act like a set gel when at rest and to flow when agitated, as through whisking, stirring, or blending. This can be a very nice effect, especially for sauces you want to coat food with or for purees that need extra body. This is a common property in fluid or sheared gels.

THE GELLING PROCESS

Even though there are lots of different kinds of gels, most of the time a similar process is used to create them. For instructions for a specific ingredient you can see the chapter for it from the section on Ingredients.

Dispersion

Typically, the first step is to disperse the gelling agent in the liquid you want to gel. Dispersion is simply the act of evenly distributing the ingredient throughout the liquid. This will ensure a gel of even strength.

A good example of dispersion gone wrong is when you try to add flour to a hot liquid. Instead of a smooth gravy you get lumps where the flour gelled together. Proper dispersion of the flour, usually using a water slurry or fat-based roux, eliminates the lumps.

Depending on the ingredient you may have to use a hot, cold, acidic, or other liquid for proper dispersion. For some ingredients a whisk or spoon will work fine, others will need the stronger shearing forces of an immersion or standing blender.

One exception to the rule of dispersing first is gelatin. It is hydrated, or "bloomed" first, before being dispersed.

Hydration

Once the gelling agent has been fully dispersed it needs to hydrate. Hydration is basically the process of absorbing water, or another liquid, and swelling. This absorption of liquid, in conjunction with other processes, causes the thickening of the mixture, creating a molecular mesh that traps water[7].

Depending on the gelling agent and the liquid being used, hydration will occur at different temperatures and over different time frames. Many ingredients will need to be heated for hydration to occur, like flour and agar.

Gelling or Setting

The final stage is when the liquid actually gels. Many gelling agents will gel at a specific temperature, others may gel at any temperature. This process can take anywhere from a few minutes to many hours.

Other Gel Considerations

Gelling Raw Ingredients

Sometimes you do not want to bring the liquid you are gelling to a boil. In order to hydrate a gelling agent that must be heated you have two options.

You can disperse and hydrate the gelling agent in a small amount of the liquid and blend the rest of the liquid into it after hydration. You can also disperse and hydrate the gelling agent in water and blend the liquid into that.

Either way, the temperature will drop quickly and some gelling agents, such as agar, will begin to set faster than usual. Warming up the liquid as much as you can is advised for better dispersion once the gelling agent has hydrated.

Water Impurities

Due to the way many of these ingredients create their molecular webs the chemicals in your water can affect the gelling power of your dishes. If you have water that has a high mineral content, or are consistently having trouble with your gels it might be worth experimenting with filtered, spring, or distilled water. It won't always fix the problem but it will at least eliminate one variable from the equation.

Hot vs Cold

Different gelling agents create gels that can withstand a wide variety of temperatures. Be sure to pick a gelling ingredient that meets the needs of the dish you are preparing. For instance, gelatin melts just

above room temperature so it cannot be used with hot preparations while agar gels can be heated up to around 80°C / 176°F before it melts.

Gelling Ingredients

There are many different gelling ingredients. This book focuses on several different modernist ingredients that we found to be easily accessible and simple to use. Below is a short description of the gelling agents we cover in depth. For specific uses of each one, as well as more recipes, please see its chapter in the Ingredients section.

Agar

Agar creates brittle gels and it must be brought to a boil to hydrate. It sets at room temperature and can be heated to 80°C / 175°F before melting. You can also add locust bean gum to agar gels to make them more elastic.

Carrageenan: Iota

Iota carrageenan creates elastic gels and is especially effective with dairy products. It is often used in custards or puddings.

It must be heated to hydrate then cooled to set the gel. Once gelled it can be reheated several degrees above the gelling temperature before melting.

Carrageenan: Kappa

Kappa carrageenan can be used to create firm, brittle gels and is especially effective at gelling dairy-based liquids. To gel, the liquid must contain either calcium or potassium that is free to bind with the kappa carrageenan.

It must be heated to hydrate then cooled to set the gel. Once gelled it can be reheated several degrees above the gelling temperature before melting.

Gelatin

Gelatin forms elastic gels that can't be raised much above room temperature. Gelatin has to be dispersed in hot liquid and sets at room temperature or below.

Methylcellulose

Methylcellulose has the uncommon ability to gel as it heats, and melt as it cools. There are many different types of methylcellulose available for a variety of uses.

Sodium Alginate

Sodium alginate is commonly used in spherification because of its ability to gel in the presence of calcium ions. It can be dispersed and hydrated at almost any temperature and the gels are very heat tolerant.

Other Gelling Agents

There are many other gelling agents we do not cover in depth but can be found in the Other Ingredients chapter such as lambda carrageenan, gellan, and pectin.

This is a nice and basic recipe for agar gels. It is brittle and has a medium firmness to it. I use pineapple juice here but almost any fruit juice will work great.

For the mold you can just use a tupperware container or get more creative and use one of the mold shapes we cover in the following section of this chapter.

Tools Needed

Agar
Immersion blender
A scale with small gram measurements
Small flat bottom mold or other container

Ingredients

300 grams pineapple juice
3 grams agar, 1.0%

Get your molds out and set up. The gel will set quickly so having them ready is crucial.

Add 150 grams of the pineapple juice to a small pot. Add the agar and blend well with an immersion blender. Bring to a boil and let simmer for 3 to 5 minutes. Add the remaining pineapple juice and blend well with the immersion blender.

Pour the liquid into the mold and let cool at room temperature. You can place the mold in an ice bath or in the refrigerator for quicker setting. Once it cools you can continue on or place it covered in the refrigerator overnight.

Once you are ready to use the gel, turn it out onto a cutting board. Cut the gel into the shapes you desire using a knife or other cutting implement.

Hold covered in the refrigerator or at room temperature until ready to serve. The cubes will remain a gel as long as they stay below 80°C / 176°F. They will last covered in the refrigerator for a few days but will slowly dry out over time.

These elastic agar gels are great as a snack or served as a garnish on pork chops. For a garnish I like to cut them into thin ribbons or small cubes.

For the mold you can just use a tupperware container or get more creative and use one of the mold shapes we cover in the next section of this chapter.

Tools Needed
Agar
Locust bean gum
Immersion blender
A scale with small gram measurements
Small flat bottom mold or other container

Ingredients
300 grams apple cider
1.5 grams agar, 0.5%
0.75 grams locust bean gum, 0.25%

Get your molds out and set up. The gel will set quickly so having them ready is crucial.

Add the apple cider to a small pot. Sprinkle in the agar and locust bean gum and blend well with an immersion blender. Bring to a boil and let simmer for 3 to 5 minutes while stirring occasionally.

Pour the liquid into the mold and let cool at room temperature. You can place the mold in an ice bath or in the refrigerator for quicker setting. Once it cools you can continue on or place it covered in the refrigerator overnight.

Once you are ready to use the gel, turn it out onto a cutting board. Cut the gel into the shapes you desire using a knife or other cutting implement.

Hold covered in the refrigerator or at room temperature until ready to serve. The cubes will remain a gel as long as they stay below 80°C / 176°F. They will last covered in the refrigerator for a few days but will slowly dry out over time.

Iota Carrageenan Herbed Custard

You can infuse milk or cream with many different flavors before gelling them with iota carrageenan. In this recipe I combine rosemary, thyme, and sage to create an herbal custard. It is great as an accompaniment with steak or roasted chicken.

Tools Needed

Iota carrageenan
Immersion blender
Molds or setting containers
Chinois
A scale with small gram measurements

Ingredients

1 teaspoon whole coriander
1 teaspoon whole peppercorns
½ teaspoon whole cumin
½ teaspoon whole cloves
500 grams milk, about 2 cups
3 tablespoons rosemary
2 tablespoons thyme
2 tablespoons sage
Salt and pepper
5 grams iota carrageenan, 1%

Place a small pan over medium heat. Add the coriander, peppercorns, cumin, and cloves and toast until fragrant, just a few minutes.

Pour the milk into a pot and add the herbs and toasted spices. Heat over medium-high heat, stirring occasionally to prevent scorching, and bring to a boil. Once it boils, blend with an immersion blender until slightly pureed. Remove from the heat and let steep for 20 to 30 minutes. Salt and pepper to taste.

Strain the milk, preferably through a chinois for the finest texture. Add the iota carrageenan and blend well with an immersion blender. Bring to a boil and blend for 30 to 60 seconds. Remove from the heat and pour into molds.

Let cool at room temperature, or in an ice bath, then place in the refrigerator to finish setting.

Once fully set the gel can be turned out and cut into any shapes desired. The gel should last for several days covered in the refrigerator.

CARRAGEENAN CINNAMON CUSTARD

For this recipe we use a mix of iota and kappa carrageenan. Iota carrageenan creates elastic gels and kappa carrageenan creates brittle gels. Using both results in a more balanced texture than using a single carrageenan.

We infuse the cream with cinnamon as well as some other spices for their background notes. It can be served cold with ice cream or it can be heated slightly and served with warm apple pie.

Tools Needed

Iota carrageenan
Kappa carrageenan
Immersion blender
Molds or setting containers
Chinois
A scale with small gram measurements

Ingredients

1 teaspoon whole coriander
1 teaspoon allspice
½ teaspoon whole cloves
½ teaspoon fennel
500 grams milk, about 2 cups
5 cinnamon sticks
1.5 grams iota carrageenan, 0.3%
1.0 grams kappa carrageenan, 0.2%

Place a small pan over medium heat. Add the coriander, allspice, cloves, and fennel and toast until fragrant, just a few minutes.

Pour the milk into a pot and add the cinnamon and toasted spices. Heat over medium-high heat, stirring occasionally to prevent scorching, and bring to a boil. Once it boils remove it from the heat and let steep for 20 to 30 minutes.

Strain the milk, preferably through a chinois for the finest texture. Add the iota and kappa carrageenan and blend well with an immersion blender. Bring to a boil and blend for 30 to 60 seconds. Remove from the heat and pour into molds.

Let cool at room temperature, or in an ice bath, then place in the refrigerator to finish setting.

Once fully set the gel can be turned out and cut into any shapes desired. The gel should last for several days covered in the refrigerator.

Jell-O shots are a favorite party snack and these help showcase how gelatin creates an elastic gel. This recipe uses a pretty standard mojito recipe but you can use any recipe you prefer, or even a pre-made mix.

Be sure you bloom and disperse the gelatin in water instead of the alcohol or you could burn all the alcohol off when you heat it.

You can let it set in any container, including tupperware, or use fancy molds or ice cube trays to make interesting shapes.

Tools Needed

Gelatin
Whisk
Chinois or strainer
Mold or container for setting

Ingredients

120 grams sugar
20 mint leaves, coarsely chopped
320 grams water
8 gelatin sheets or 2 powdered gelatin packets, 1.5%
350 grams rum
150 grams lime juice, preferably fresh

First make the mint simple syrup. Place sugar, mint, and 150 grams of water in a pot. Heat to a boil, stirring, and cook until the sugar is dissolved. Set aside and let cool. Pour through a strainer.

Add the reserved water and the gelatin to a pot. Let the gelatin bloom in the water for 5 to 10 minutes.

Once the gelatin has bloomed, add the mint simple syrup and heat over medium to medium-high heat while stirring until the gelatin dissolves completely. Remove the pot from the heat.

Add the rum and lime juice, and whisk to combine. Pour the mixture into your mold or container and let cool. Once it has cooled slightly place it in the refrigerator for several hours.

After it is fully set you can unmold it and cut it into any shapes you like. Store them in the refrigerator until serving.

Shaping Gels

One of the most interesting uses of gels is the different shapes you can create with them. From standard cubes to spheres and noodles, the shapes help add visual appeal to dishes.

Serving Dishes

For soft gels, it is best to have them set directly in the dish you want to serve them in. Soft gels have a tendency to break apart if you try to cut or unmold them. You can also set harder gels in the serving dishes and it can have a great visual appeal, especially if you are using glass serving dishes.

Free Form

The easiest way to shape gels is by setting it in a block and then cutting it into the shapes you prefer. I will often use a tupperware container that the gel will fill to the final height I am looking for, typically 6 mm to 25 mm / ¼" to 1". I can then cut it into cubes with a knife, or for harder gels I can even use cookie cutters for a wide range of shapes.

Sheets

For many elastic gels, you can set them in a thin layer, less than 3 mm / ⅛" thick on a flat, plastic surface. This creates a flexible sheet you can drape over or wrap around foods.

Molds

Another easy way to set creatively shaped gels it to use molds. These can be in the form of silicon or plastic molds. There are ice cube trays you can use that come in a wide variety of shapes and sizes. In addition, there are hemispherical and spherical molds of different sizes that can be used for interesting shapes.

Noodles

Another interesting presentation is making gel noodles. These have many uses but are typically used as a garnish. To make the gel noodles the warm gel base is pushed into plastic tubing, usually using a plastic syringe, and then placed in ice water to cool. Be sure you use elastic gels when making noodles otherwise they will fall apart when being handled.

Pearls

Round beads of gel always add some great visual appeal to plates. There are a few ways to make them but I've found the easiest is to make them in cold oil.

Place a glass of oil in the freeze for about an hour so it thickens slightly. You can use any type of oil but canola, vegetable, or olive oil works well.

Make the gel base and then drip it into the oil. While the gel is falling to the bottom of the oil it is in a spherical shape and because the oil is cold the gel will set before it makes it to the bottom.

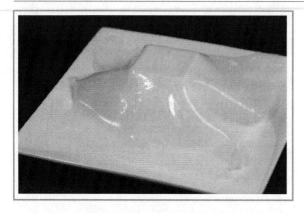

These gel sheets are very versatile. They can be cut into wide strips and used as a wrapper for sushi. You can cut them into squares and use them as a pseudo wonton wrapper. You can also just drape them over vegetables or stir fried meat.

Tools Needed

Agar
Gelatin
Standing or immersion blender
Flat, plastic surface
A scale with small gram measurements

Ingredients

250 grams orange juice, preferably fresh
50 mm / 2" piece of ginger, peeled and roughly
    chopped
1 teaspoon red pepper flakes
3.0 gram agar, 1.2%
2 gelatin sheets or ½ powdered gelatin packet,
    1.4%

If using sheet gelatin, place it in a bowl of cold water to bloom. If using powdered gelatin combine it with 50 grams of water and 100 grams of orange juice. Let the gelatin bloom for 5 to 10 minutes.

While the gelatin is blooming place the remaining orange juice, ginger, and red pepper flakes in a pot. Bring to a simmer, remove from the heat and let steep for 10 minutes. Strain the orange juice and return to the pot.

Sprinkle in the agar and mix well with an immersion blender. Bring to a simmer while stirring occasionally. Let simmer for 3 to 5 minutes then remove from the heat.

If using powdered gelatin, whisk in the water-orange juice mixture and let dissolve. If using sheet gelatin, squeeze out the water and add the sheets, whisking them into the agar mixture until they dissolve.

Spoon some of the gel base onto the flat, plastic surface, tipping the surface until the gel evenly coats it. Let the sheet set, it should only take a few minutes, and then the gel sheet will be ready to use.

These mango noodles are a great visual touch to dishes. I like to serve them draped over ice cream or a sundae but they can also be heated and served with jerk pork or as a garnish on an Asian citrus salad.

We add the locust bean gum to this recipe so the resulting gel will be more elastic than a typical agar gel would be. This will help the noodles hold together and keep their form.

Tools Needed
Agar
Locust bean gum
Standing or immersion blender
Plastic syringe and tubing
A scale with small gram measurements

Ingredients
300 grams mango juice
1.0 grams agar, 0.33%
1.0 grams locust bean gum, 0.33%

Prepare an ice bath to set the gel in.

Place the mango juice in a pot. Sprinkle in the agar and locust bean gum and mix well with an immersion blender. Bring to a simmer while stirring occasionally. Let simmer for 3 to 5 minutes.

Fill a syringe with the gel base, attach it to a section of tubing, and then push the gel into the tubing. Remove the filled tubing and place it into the ice bath. Once the gel has set, 2 to 5 minutes, fill the syringe with air, reattach it to the set tubing, and push the gel out.

Repeat for as many noodles as you want. You can also make several noodles at once if you have multiple sections of tubing.

Once the noodles are made they are ready to be served or can be refrigerated, covered, for several hours.

Gel pearls are a great way to add texture and visual appeal to a dish. You can use almost any liquid to make them but here we use balsamic vinegar for an acidic, yet sweet, flavor. These go great as a garnish on a salad, a topping for steak, or even on fresh mozzarella and tomatoes.

Tools Needed

Agar
Standing or immersion blender
Plastic syringe, eye dropper, or squeeze bottle
A scale with small gram measurements

Ingredients

200 grams balsamic vinegar
2 grams agar, 1.0%

Place a glass or bowl of olive oil in the freezer for 30 to 60 minutes.

Place the balsamic vinegar in a pot. Sprinkle in the agar and mix well with an immersion blender. Bring to a simmer while stirring occasionally. Let simmer for 3 to 5 minutes.

Using the syringe, squeeze bottle or eye dropper drip the gel base into the oil. You can do many pearls at the same time. Once the gel has set you can take them out with a slotted spoon and rinse them in a container of plain water. Repeat for as many pearls as you want.

Once the pearls have been made the are ready to be served or can be refrigerated, covered, for several days.

FLUID GELS

Fluid gels are a special type of gel that behave as both a gel and a liquid. They may look like a gel and taste like a liquid, or look like a liquid but suspend other particles like a gel does.

The best known example of a fluid gel is ketchup. It looks and acts like a gel in the bottle and will not come out despite your best efforts. Then suddenly, the shear forces are enough and the gel turns into a liquid and flows quickly all over your plate.

When to Use Fluid Gels

Fluid gels have many of the same uses as thickened liquids but there are some specific differences between them.

Thicker Liquids

Unlike many thickeners, such as xanthan gum, fluid gels can be made very thick without developing bad textures. This helps create sauces with the consistency of ketchup or even pudding without developing unfavorable mouthfeel. If you tried to use xanthan gum to thicken the same amount if would develop an unappealing mucus-like texture.

Stays in Place

Because fluid gels act like a gel when they are stationary they tend to stay put on the plate better. This is nice if you have different sauces for different items, or if the sauces are a separate, decorative element. Also, unlike thickened liquids, they thin out when eaten, so the texture in the mouth can be different than the texture on the plate.

Particle Suspension

The suspension of particles can be accomplished both with a fluid gel and a thickened liquid. However, a thickened liquid will feel thick in the mouth while the fluid gel will feel thin and fluid. This is why many beverages with particles in them, such as fruit juices and flavored milks, use fluid gels instead of thickened liquids, they are more palatable.

Fluid Gel Process

Fluid gels are very easy to create. You first make a standard gel using one of a subset of the above gelling agents. You can adjust the initial thickness of the fluid gel by changing the concentration of the gelling ingredient.

Once the gel sets you puree it in a standing blender or with an immersion blender until smooth. You can change the thickness of the pureed gel by adding xanthan gum to thicken it or liquid to thin it out.

Fluid Gel Containers

I try to use a container that works well with my immersion blender so I can blend it directly in the container, but any container will work. If you need it to gel more quickly, try to use a container that is wide and flat, so the gel will not be as thick and will set faster.

Fluid Gel Ingredients

A few of the gelling agents work well for the creation of fluid gels. I've found best results for cold gels with agar, iota and kappa carrageenan, and gelatin. For hot gels, agar is really the only ingredient in this book that can hold up to the heat. Gellan, which we don't cover in depth, is also commonly used.

Pre-Made Fluid Gel

If you find yourself making fluid gels on a regular basis or want to gel raw ingredients, you can sacrifice some flavor by using pre-made fluid gels. Simply make a gel with water and 1% agar and let it set. It will last covered in the refrigerator for a week or two.

When you want to turn a liquid into a fluid gel you puree it with some of the pre-made fluid gel. Just start with a small amount and continue adding more until the liquid is the texture you prefer.

Because of the water content it will dilute the liquid some but the convenience can be worth it.

Papaya Pudding

Papaya has a nice, mild flavor that can complement fish and lighter poultry. We turn it into a pudding here to add body and texture to it.

Tools Needed

Agar
Standing or immersion blender
A scale with small gram measurements

Ingredients

400 grams papaya juice
42 grams honey, about 2 tablespoons
4 grams agar, 1.0%
0.4-1.6 grams xanthan gum, optional, 0.1% - 0.4%

Blend the papaya juice and agar together.

Place the papaya mixture into a pot and bring to a boil. Let simmer for 3 to 5 minutes. Pour the papaya mixture into a container and let it completely set.

Once it is set, cube the gel. Puree the papaya gel using a blender, immersion blender, or food processor until smooth. Add some water if you need to thin it, or some xanthan gum to thicken it.

Once it reaches the desired consistency it is ready to be served.

This shows how the same traditional ingredients can be transformed by using a different modernist ingredient. It uses the same ingredients for the Bourbon Glaze in the Thickening chapter but replaces the xanthan gum with agar. It's a little more involved but the result is a fantastic, thick sauce that will last in the refrigerator for up to a week..

Even though there are several steps, they are all very easy and quick to do. First, we combine all the ingredients and gel them. Then we blend the gel to make a fluid gel, basically a flavorful, thick sauce.

You can change the final thickness of the sauce by changing the amount of agar you use.

Tools Needed
Agar
Xanthan gum, optional
Immersion blender
Immersion or standing blender
A scale with small gram measurements

Ingredients
207 grams bourbon whiskey, about 1 cup
110 grams brown sugar, about ½ cup
140 grams ketchup, about ½ cup
10 grams Worcester sauce, about 2 teaspoons
5 grams liquid smoke, about 1 teaspoon
60 grams apple juice, about ¼ cup
12 grams lemon juice, about 1 tablespoon
1 teaspoon chopped garlic
½ teaspoon cayenne pepper
¼ teaspoon dry mustard
Salt and pepper
4 grams agar, 0.75%
0.5-2.2 grams xanthan gum, optional, 0.1-04%

Add all of the ingredients except the agar and xanthan gum to a pot over medium-high heat. Bring to a simmer, stirring occasionally.

Taste the sauce for seasoning and adjust as needed. Once the sauce tastes balanced it is ready to be gelled.

Sprinkle in the agar and blend well with the immersion blender. Let it simmer for 3 to 5 minutes and then pour out into a container for it to set.

Once the gel has fully set, roughly chop it into cubes and place it a blender or a container that works well with your immersion blender. Blend the gel well until it becomes a thick, smooth sauce. You can add water to thin it out or some xanthan gum to thicken it if needed.

It can now be used as is or refrigerated for later use. It can be heated up to 80°C / 175°F before it will break down.

TERIYAKI SAUCE

Teriyaki sauce is one of my favorite sauces. This sauce doesn't take very long to make, besides letting the gel cool.

Tools Needed

Agar
Xanthan gum, optional
Immersion blender
Immersion or standing blender
Chinois, optional
A scale with small gram measurements

Ingredients

80 grams soy sauce, about ⅓ cup
60 grams hoisin sauce, about ¼ cup
50 grams brown sugar, about ¼ cup
100 grams diced pineapple, about ½ cup
1 fresh red chile, diced
2 garlic cloves, diced
1 tablespoon grated ginger
45 grams rice vinegar, about 3 tablespoons
1.7 grams agar, 0.5%
0.3-1.2 grams xanthan gum, optional, 0.1-0.4%

Add all of the ingredients except the agar and xanthan gum to a pot over medium-high heat. Bring to a simmer, stirring occasionally.

Taste the sauce for seasoning and adjust as needed. Once the sauce tastes balanced it is ready to be gelled. For a more refined sauce you can strain it with a chinois before gelling it.

Sprinkle in the agar and blend well with the immersion blender. Let it simmer for 3 to 5 minutes and then pour out into a container for it to set.

Once the gel has fully set roughly chop it into cubes and place it a blender or a container that works well with your immersion blender. Blend the gel well until it becomes a thick, smooth sauce. You can add water to thin it out or some xanthan gum to thicken it if needed.

It can now be used as is or refrigerated for later use. It can be heated up to 80°C / 175°F before it will break down.

Smoky bacon and creamy blue cheese is a great pairing. We first infuse cream with bacon and then add blue cheese and iota carrageenan to gel it.

It's great as a topping on grilled steaks or even as a dip for vegetables.

Tools Needed

Iota carrageenan
Standing or immersion blender
Chinois
A scale with small gram measurements

Ingredients

10 strips bacon, cooked and diced
375 grams heavy cream, about 1½ cups
Salt and pepper
125 grams blue cheese, about ½ cup
1 gram iota carrageenan, 0.2%
0.5-2 grams xanthan gum, optional, 0.1% - 0.4%

Pour the cream into a pot and add the bacon. Bring to a simmer and puree with an immersion blender until pureed well. Remove from the heat and let steep for 20 to 30 minutes. Salt and pepper to taste.

For a finer texture you can strain the cream through a chinois. Return the cream to the pot, add the iota carrageenan and blend well with an immersion blender. Bring to a simmer. Add the blue cheese and blend until mixed well. Remove from the heat and pour into a container for it to set.

Let cool at room temperature, or in an ice bath, then place in the refrigerator to finish setting.

Once fully set cut the gel into cubes and puree with a standing or immersion blender, or food processor until nice and smooth. If needed, you can add some water to thin it, or some xanthan gum to thicken it.

After it is pureed it is ready to be served.

LOW TEMPERATURE COOKING

For a more detailed look at sous vide, the equipment needed, and the specifics of the process you can view our free Beginning Sous Vide guide on our website.

You can find them on our website at:
www.cookingsousvide.com/beginning-sous-vide-guide.html

History of Sous Vide

Sous vide, or low temperature cooking, is the process of cooking food at a very tightly controlled temperature, normally the temperature the food will be served at. This is a departure from traditional cooking methods that use high heat to cook the food, which must be removed at the exact moment it reaches the desired temperature.

Sous vide was first used as an upscale culinary technique in kitchens in France in the 1970s and traditionally is the process of cooking vacuum sealed food in a low temperature water bath. This process helps to achieve texture and doneness not found in other cooking techniques, as well as introducing many conveniences for a professional kitchen. Sous vide has slowly been spreading around the world in professional kitchens everywhere and is finally making the jump to home kitchens.

As sous vide has become more popular and moved to the home kitchen the term now encompasses both traditional "under vacuum" sous vide and also low temperature cooking. Some preparations rely on the vacuum pressure to change the texture of the food but in most cases the benefits of sous vide are realized in the controlled, low temperature cooking process. This means that fancy vacuum sealers can be set aside for home sealers or even ziploc bags.

How it Works

The basic concept of sous vide cooking is that food should be cooked at the temperature it will be served at. For instance, if you are cooking a steak to medium rare, you want to serve it at 131°F / 55°C.

With traditional cooking methods you would normally cook it on a hot grill or oven at around 400°F-500°F / 200°C-260°C and pull it off at the right moment when the middle has reached 131°F / 55°C. This results in a "bulls-eye effect" of burnt meat on the outside turning to medium rare in the middle. This steak cooked sous vide would be cooked at 131°F / 55°C for several hours. This will result in the entire piece of meat being a perfectly cooked medium rare. The steak would then usually be quickly seared at high heat to add the flavorful, browned crust to it.

There are two basic components to sous vide cooking at home: temperature and time. Each one of these can affect the end quality, texture, and taste of sous vide dishes. Understanding how they affect the food is one of the most important things to learn as you begin sous vide cooking.

Temperature

All sous vide cooking is done at temperatures below the boiling point of water and normally not above 185°F / 85°C. You usually cook the food at the temperature you want it served at, so most settings are between 120°F / 49°C and 185°F / 85°C, depending on the food being prepared.

While the range of temperature used in sous vide is much less variable than for traditional cooking, the precise control of the temperature is of great importance. When you set your oven at 400°F it actually fluctuates about 50 degrees, sending it between 375°F and 425°F, which is fine when cooking at high temperatures. When cooking sous vide, the temperature of the water determines the doneness of your food, so a 50°F fluctuation would result in over-cooked food. Most sous vide machines fluctuate less than 1°F and the best are less than 0.1°F.

This precision is why many sous vide machines are very expensive. However, there are many more home machines available in the last few years, some good do-it-yourself kits, and even some ways to accomplish "accurate enough" sous vide on the cheap[8].

Time

Cooking tenderizes food by breaking down its internal structure. This process happens faster at higher temperatures. Because sous vide is done at such low temperatures the cooking time needs to be increased to achieve the same tenderization as traditional techniques.

Also, your window of time to perfectly cooked food is much longer than with traditional cooking methods because you are cooking the food at the temperature you want it to end up at, rather than a higher temperature. This also allows you to leave food in the water bath even after it is done since keeping it at this temperature does not dry out the food, up to several hours longer for tougher cuts of meat. However, be careful not to take this concept too far as food can still become overcooked by sous vide, many times without showing it externally.

Temperature and Time Together

The power of sous vide cooking comes from precisely controlling both temperature and time. This is important because of the way meat reacts to different temperatures.

At 120°F / 49°C meat slowly begins to tenderize as the protein myosin begins to coagulate and the connective tissue in the meat begins to break down. As the temperature increases so does the speed of tenderization.

However, meat also begins to lose its moisture above 140°F / 60°C as the heat causes the collagen in the cells to shrink and wring out the moisture. This happens very quickly over 150°F / 65.5°C and the meat becomes completely dried out above 160°F / 71°C.

Many tough cuts of meat are braised or roasted for a long period of time so the meat can fully tenderize, but because of the high temperatures they can easily become dried out. Using sous vide allows you to hold the meat below the 140°F / 60°C barrier long enough for the slower tenderization process to be effective. This results in very tender meat that is still moist and not overcooked.

Basic Sous Vide Technique

Sous vide is actually a very easy and convenient method of cooking. First season the food and seal it in a plastic bag. Place it into a water bath preheated to the temperature you want the food to end up. Cook it from one hour up to several days, depending on the type of food. Remove it from the bag and briefly sear it for flavor and texture.

While there are variations within each dish, almost every sous vide meal follows the same steps. Here is a more detailed look at those steps.

Flavor the Food

Just like many traditional methods, you often times flavor the food before cooking it. This can be as simple as a sprinkling of salt and pepper or as complicated as adding an elaborate sauce, spice rub, or even smoking the food. Depending on the type of seasoning it can either be rubbed directly onto the food itself or added into the pouch with the food.

If you are using a normal home vacuum sealer and want to add more than a little liquid, freeze the liquid before adding it to the pouch. This way the process of vacuum sealing will not suck out the liquid. Otherwise, you can normally use food grade ziploc bags to seal food with liquids.

When seasoning for sous vide most typical spices and flavorings can be used with a few exceptions:

- Fresh soft herbs like basil or parsley will not hold up well

- Fresh garlic or ginger can become bitter

- Vinegars can become more pronounced

- If you are cooking for more than 8 hours then you might not want to salt meat right away as it can draw out some moisture

You can also re-season the food when it comes out of the water bath. This is a good way to apply traditional rubs whose flavors you want on the surface of the food but not on the inside.

Seal the Food

Once the seasoning and food have been added to the pouch, remove the air and seal it closed. Removing the air results in closer contact between the food and the water in the water bath. This helps to facilitate quicker cooking since water transfers heat more efficiently than air.

Sealing the food can be done with anything from ziplocs or food grade plastic wrap to a FoodSaver Vacuum Sealer or even a chambered vacuum sealer.

Some vacuum sealers have different strengths of vacuum to seal the bag and can be used to affect the texture of some types of food.

Even though "sous vide" means "under vacuum" the vacuum sealing of foods is not critical to the sous vide process in any way. Any food-grade, sealable plastic bag works well. I often use Ziploc brand freezer bags and they work great.

When using non-vacuum sealed plastic bags you should use the water displacement method, also known as the Archimedes principal[9], where you hold the bag underwater with just the top sticking out before sealing it. The pressure of the water forces out the air and creates a tight seal. When done properly this is almost as good as using a weak vacuum sealer and will work great for most low-temperature sous vide cooking.

Heat the Water

Simply bring the water bath up to the temperature you will cook at. This water bath will normally be the same temperature that you will want your food to end up at.

Depending on the type of heat regulator, you may be able to have the food in the water while it heats. For others, it is best to preheat the water before placing the food in it due to early fluctuations in temperature.

The most difficult part of sous vide cooking has traditionally been the temperature control. Maintaining a precise temperature is critical, both from a quality and a safety standpoint.

For people wanting to experiment with sous vide, temperature control can be done with a large pot of water on a stove with a thermometer or by pouring heated water into a beer cooler.

For anyone that wants to use sous vide regularly there are also many options for home cooks. I personally use the SousVideMagic, Sous Vide Supreme, and PolyScience Professional[10]. They range from $150 for the SousVideMagic, which hooks up to an existing crock pot, to $800 for the PolyScience unit, which is used in many professional kitchens[11].

Cook the Food

Put the food pouch in the water and let it cook for the amount of time specified in the recipe or on the Time and Temperature chart. For items that are cooked for longer amounts of time it can be good to rotate the food every 6 to 10 hours, especially if you are using less precise sous vide equipment.

At some higher temperatures the sous vide pouches can float due to air released from the food. If that happens you might have to use a plate or bowl to weight them down.

Finish the Dish

To get a good finish and texture to your food, especially meats, it is usually advisable to quickly sear the meat. This is usually done in hot pan, on a grill, or with a culinary blow torch. Some meals also call for other methods of finishing the food, such as breading and deep-frying for chicken.

You can also quickly chill the food in an ice bath which is ½ ice and ½ water and then refrigerate or freeze the food for later re-heating.

Choose Your Finishing Method

One of the key things in most sous vide dishes is the finishing method used. The different methods add their flavors and textures to the meat. Depending on what the dish is and what you are trying to accomplish you will want to choose one of the following methods.

Pan Frying

Pan frying or pan searing is the most common method of finishing sous vide meats. It can usually be used instead of grilling with only a slight loss of the grilling flavor. It's usually done in oil in a hot pan on the stove. The meat is left on just long enough to brown before being removed.

Grilling

Grilling is a great way to finish meat since it adds the smoky flavor and the grill marks so common in grilled foods. For most foods it and pan frying are interchangeable.

Torching

Many people that use sous vide often will invest in a good butane food torch for searing their food. A common torch is the Iwatani torch[12].

Roasting

Roasting or broiling are not as common as the other methods but they can be a great way to finish crusts or sear the top and sides of sous vide meat. It is normally done at 450°F / 232°C or under the broiler. You can also do this on your grill by using very high, indirect heat.

Smoking

Some recipes call for food to be smoked either before or after you cook them. You can still accomplish this by smoking it after you remove the food from the sous vide bath. For longer times or cold smoking it can be better to smoke the meat beforehand to minimize the time the food is in the danger zone.

Sous Vide Safety

Sous vide is a new and largely untested method of cooking. It potentially carries many inherent health risks that may not be fully understood. We have done our best to provide the latest information and what is currently understood about this form of cooking.

However, we feel that anyone undertaking sous vide cooking, or any other method of cooking, should fully inform themselves about any and all risks associated with it and come to their own conclusions about its safety. Following anything in this book could possibly make you or your guests sick and should only be done if you are fully aware of the potential risks and complications.

There are two main concerns when it comes to sous vide cooking; they are pathogens and the dangers of cooking in plastic.

Pathogens, Bacteria and Salmonella

One large safety concern with sous vide that has been studied in great detail deals with the propagation of bacteria at various temperatures, especially salmonella. Salmonella only thrive in a certain range of temperatures, from about 40°F / 4°C to 130°F / 54°C, often referred to as the "danger zone".

This danger zone is why we refrigerate our foods until an hour or so before we are ready to cook them. It is also why we cook our foods to specific temperatures before we eat them.

The biggest misconception about bacteria and the danger zone is that any food in the temperature range is not safe and as soon as you move above 130°F / 54°C the food instantly becomes safe. The truth is that the bacteria begin to die in direct relation to the temperature they are exposed to.

The best way to visualize this is to think about how we humans react to heat. We do fine in climates where the temperature is below 100°F / 38°C. However, once it begins to climb around 110°F / 43°C or 120°F / 49°C you begin to hear about deaths in the news due to heat stroke. If the temperature were to raise to 200°F / 93°C stepping outside for more than a few seconds would kill you.

Bacteria behave in the exact same way. They begin to die at around 130°F / 54°C to 135°F / 57°C and 165°F / 74°C just about instantly kills them. You can see this in the chart below, based on the USDA safety data[13]. At 136°F / 57.7°C it takes about 63 minutes for your food to be safe and at 146°F / 63.3°C it only takes 7 minutes to become safe.

This concept is why the USDA recommends that chicken is cooked to 165°F / 73.8°C, because at that temperature it takes only a few seconds for enough bacteria to die to achieve acceptable safety levels. In comparison, at 136°F / 57.7°C it takes 63.3 minutes at that temperature to achieve the same safety level, something that is virtually impossible using traditional cooking methods. Using sous vide makes it possible to heat chicken and other meats to an internal temperature of as low as 130°F / 54°C and hold it there long enough to kill the bacteria.

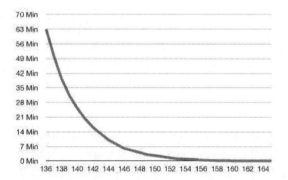

Please remember that this is assuming that your thermometer is exact and the water temperature is completely steady. I recommend always cooking foods at a little higher than the minimum temperature and a little longer than the minimum cooking time in order to account for any variance in temperature your equipment causes.

For more explanations of how this works you can reference the excellent guides by Douglas Baldwin or Serious Eats mentioned in our Resources chapter.

Plastic Safety

Another main concern of sous vide is cooking in plastic and whether or not this is a dangerous practice. Many scientists and chefs believe that cooking in food grade plastic at these low temperatures does not pose any risk. The temperature is about equivalent to leaving a bottle of water in your car, or in a semi during transport, in summer.

However, I find it hard to believe that we know everything about how plastic reacts to heat, water, our bodies, and the environment. As such, I encourage you to read up on the safety of plastic in sous vide and plastic in general and come to your own conclusions about the safety of using these techniques or consuming products packaged or shipped in plastic.

Pre-Bath Time: 15 Minutes
Cooking Time: 1 to 2 Days
Finishing Time: 30 Minutes
Temperature: 131°F / 55°C
Serves: 4 to 6

Pre-Bath Ingredients

For the Roast
2-3 pounds chuck roast
3 tablespoons achiote paste
Pepper

Finishing Ingredients

For the Polenta
2 tablespoons butter
2 jalapenos, diced
¼ cup milk
2 cups chicken stock
Water as per the directions on the polenta
  package
1 ⅓ cups quick cooking polenta
2 tablespoon chopped fresh cilantro
Salt and pepper

Achiote is a richly flavored paste from Central and South America made from annatto seeds mixed with other spices such as coriander, oregano, cumin, and garlic. You can find it on the international aisle of many grocery stores. We pair it with a creamy polenta with jalapenos in it but you could also use mashed potatoes if you prefer.

Pre-Bath

Coat the roast evenly with the achiote paste then pepper it. Add the roast to the sous vide pouch then seal.

At this point you can store the pouch in the refrigerator for up to 2 days, freeze it for up to 6 months, or cook it right away.

Cooking

Preheat the water bath to 131°F / 55°C.

Place the pouch in the water bath for 1 to 2 days.

Finishing

Preheat a grill to high heat or a pan to medium-high heat.

Heat a pot over medium-high heat. Add the butter and melt. Add the jalapeno and cook for a few minutes until it softens. Add the milk, chicken stock, and enough water to bring the volume of liquid to the amount called for by the directions on the polenta package. Bring the liquid to a boil and then whisk in the polenta and cook, stirring, until it thickens. Remove from the heat.

Take the beef out of the water bath and remove it from the pouch. Pat it dry with a paper towel or dish cloth. Quickly sear the roast for 1 to 2 minutes per side, until just browned, then remove from the heat.

Portion the beef and serve it on top of the polenta.

Pre-Bath Time: 10 Minutes
Cooking Time: 1 to 3 Days
Finishing Time: 30 Minutes
Temperature: 135°F / 57°C
Serves: 4

Pre-Bath Ingredients
2-3 pounds cured, uncooked corned beef

Finishing Ingredients
8 slices rye bread
8 slices swiss cheese
About 1 cup thousand island dressing
High quality Dijon mustard
1 cup sauerkraut

Corned beef cooked with sous vide results in meat with great texture and tenderness. It is also juicier and more flavorful than many corned beefs.

In this recipe we call for it to be cooked at 135°F / 57°C which was the temperature we liked best. However, our test with the corned beef cooked at 146°F / 63.3°C was also very good. It was drier than the 135°F / 57°C meat but a bit more tender. Either temperature will result in fantastic corned beef.

Sometimes the corned beef will turn out too salty. If that is the case place it in a ziplock bag with some warm water and place back in the water bath. Over time the water in the bag will draw out the salt from the corned beef.

Pre-Bath
Place the corned beef in a sous vide pouch with any included spices then seal.

At this point you can store the pouch in the refrigerator for up to 2 days, freeze it for up to 6 months, or cook it right away.

Cooking
Preheat the water bath to 135°F / 57°C.

Place the pouch in the water bath for 1 to 3 days.

Finishing
Heat a pan over medium-high heat.

Remove the corned beef from the water bath and pat dry. Quickly sear it in the pan until just browned, about 1 to 2 minutes per side. Remove from the heat and slice into thin strips.

Brush one side of the bread slices with olive oil and toast until browned. Place the cheese on the un-toasted side of the bread and toast in a toaster oven or an oven with the broiler on until the cheese melts.

Add the thousand island dressing to four of the slices and the mustard to the other four. Pile the corned beef on the slices with mustard and top with the sauerkraut. Place the two halves together and serve.

Pre-Bath Time: 15 Minutes
Cooking Time: 3 to 6 Hours
Finishing Time: 45 Minutes
Temperature: 135°F / 57.5°C
Serves: 4

Pre-Bath Ingredients
For the Pork
1-2 pounds pork tenderloin
1 teaspoon dried sage
1 teaspoon allspice
½ teaspoon ginger
Pepper

Finishing Ingredients
For the Glaze
1 cup bourbon whiskey
½ cup brown sugar
½ cup ketchup
2 teaspoons Worcester sauce
1 teaspoon liquid smoke
¼ cup apple juice
1 tablespoon lemon juice
1 teaspoon minced garlic
½ teaspoon cayenne pepper
¼ teaspoon dry mustard
Salt and pepper

This simple recipe takes a sometimes bland pork tenderloin and adds layers of flavor with the glaze. I usually sear the pork when it is just out of the refrigerator or at room temperature. This allows me more time to develop the glaze on it.

To save time you can also skip the step of reducing the sauce and just use it after you combine all the ingredients but the flavors will not be as strong.

Pre-Bath
Mix the spices together in a bowl. Pepper the pork tenderloin, sprinkle with the spices, then place in the sous vide pouches and seal.

At this point you can store the pouch in the refrigerator for up to 2 days, freeze it for up to 6 months, or cook it right away.

Cooking
Preheat the water bath to 135°F / 57.2°C. Place the sous vide pouches in the water bath and cook for 3 to 6 hours.

Remove the pouches and place in a ½ ice - ½ water bath until chilled. You can store the pouches in the refrigerator for around 2 days or freeze them for up to 6 months.

Finishing
Preheat a grill to high heat or the broiler in the oven.

To prepare the glaze mix together all of the ingredients in a pot over medium-high heat and bring to a simmer, stirring occasionally. Cook for about 30 minutes, until it thickens some.

Take the pork out of the pouches and pat dry. Sear on the grill until grill marks form on the first side, a couple of minutes. Brush the glaze on the side facing up and turn the tenderloin. Repeat several times until it is coated with the glaze, cooking about 30 to 60 seconds per turn.

Remove from the heat, brush once more with the glaze, slice into ½" rounds and serve.

Pre-Bath Time: 15 Minutes
Cooking Time: 8 to 12 Hours
Finishing Time: 15 Minutes
Temperature: 135°F / 57.2°C
Serves: 2 to 4

Pre-Bath Ingredients
For the Ribs
2 pounds St. Louis style ribs, trimmed of excess
   fat and silverskin
1 tablespoon ground cumin
1 tablespoon garlic powder
2 dried bay leaves
1 tablespoon dried lemon peel (optional)
Pepper

Finishing Ingredients
½ cup your favorite BBQ sauce

*Ribs are a great meal to cook during the week. After
10 to 12 hours in the water bath they become very
tender and they are very quick to finish cooking. It's
also very satisfying to dig into a big plate of them
after a hard day of work.*

*I use St. Louis style ribs but baby back ribs will also
work well. You can also cook them under the broiler if
you don't want to grill them.*

Pre-Bath
Mix together all the spices except the bay
leaf in a bowl. Cut the ribs into pieces that
will easily fit into your sous vide bags.
Pepper the ribs and then coat them with the
spice mix.

Place the ribs into the sous vide pouches,
add the bay leaves, then seal. Be sure you
don't seal the ribs too tightly or the bones
may pierce the bag.

At this point you can store the pouch in the
refrigerator for up to 2 days, freeze it for up
to 6 months, or cook it right away.

Cooking
On the morning of the day you want to eat,
preheat your sous vide water bath to
135°F / 57.2°C. Place the pouch in the water
bath for 8 to 12 hours.

Finishing
Preheat a grill to high heat.

Remove the sous vide pouches from the
water bath and take the ribs out of the
pouches. Pat them dry and then coat with
the BBQ sauce.

Quickly grill the ribs just until the BBQ
sauce begins to caramelize, about 1 to 2
minutes per side. Take off the grill and
serve.

Pre-Bath Time: 15 Minutes
Cooking Time: 2 to 12 Hours
Finishing Time: 45 Minutes
Temperature: 141°F / 60.5°C
Serves: 4

Pre-Bath Ingredients
For the Chicken
4 chicken breasts
½ teaspoon garlic powder
4 sprigs fresh thyme
4 sprigs fresh rosemary
Pepper

Finishing Ingredients
For the Coating
¾ cup flour
2 teaspoons salt
1 teaspoon black pepper
2 eggs
¾ cup dried Italian bread crumbs
¼ cup grated parmesan cheese
2 tablespoons chopped parsley

For the Topping
½ cup chopped basil
8-10 ¼" slices of fresh mozzarella, or 1 cup
  shredded
4 tablespoons grated parmesan cheese

Chicken Parmigiana is one of my favorite dishes and I get it at almost every Italian restaurant I go to. Here's a simple version that you can make at home. The sous vide process ensures the chicken is cooked through and you can just focus on getting the coating nice and crispy. I love to serve this with spaghetti and marinara sauce on the side. You can also serve this in a toasted hoagie roll with marinara sauce for a chicken parm grinder, a staple on most New England menus. You can leave the chicken breasts whole or cut them in half width-wise for a higher "crust to chicken" ratio.

Note: Chicken is best when cooked for 2 to 4 hours but during the week you can get away with cooking it for up to 12 hours with just a minimal loss in moisture.

Pre-Bath
Pepper the chicken then sprinkle with the garlic powder. Place in sous vide pouches with the thyme and rosemary and seal.

At this point you can store the pouch in the refrigerator for up to 2 days, freeze it for up to 6 months, or cook it right away.

Cooking
On the morning of the day you want to eat, preheat your sous vide water bath to 141°F / 60.5°C. Place the pouch in the water bath for 2 to 12 hours.

Finishing
Preheat a pan to medium-high heat. Preheat the broiler on the oven.

First you will want to set up three stations for the breading. Combine the flour, salt, and pepper on a plate. Beat the eggs into a wide mouth bowl. Combine the bread crumbs, parmesan cheese, and parsley on another plate.

Remove the chicken from the pouches and pat dry. Dredge the chicken in the flour, then the egg, then the bread crumbs.

Add about ½" of oil to the pan and heat to about 350°F to 375°F (176°C - 190°C). Sear the dredged chicken breasts until the crust becomes golden brown, flip and repeat on the other side. Remove from the heat and set on a sheet pan.

Top each one with the basil and cover with the mozzarella and parmesan cheese. Broil in the oven until the cheese is browned and bubbly. Remove and serve.

SHRIMP POMODORO OVER LINGUINE

Pre-Bath Time: 15 Minutes
Cooking Time: 15 to 35 Minutes
Finishing Time: 30 Minutes
Temperature: 122°F / 50°C for sushi quality or
132°F / 55.6°C otherwise
Serves: 4

Pre-Bath Ingredients

For the Shrimp
20-25 medium sized shrimp, shelled and
    deveined
1 tablespoon butter
¼ teaspoon cayenne pepper, or chile powder of
    your choice
Salt and pepper

Finishing Ingredients

12 ounces linguine pasta, or pasta of your choice

For the Pomodoro Sauce
2 tablespoons olive oil
4 cloves garlic, minced
½ yellow onion, diced
1 28-ounce can of diced tomatoes
1 tablespoon butter
2 tablespoons chopped fresh basil
1 tablespoon chopped fresh oregano
Salt and pepper

For the Garnish
Parmesan cheese
1 tablespoon chopped basil
1 tablespoon lemon zest

Pomodoro sauce is a very fast tomato sauce to make. It really highlights the flavor of the tomatoes and herbs in it. I like to serve this with some fresh bread to really soak up all the sauce.

Here I call for using canned, diced tomatoes which work well but if you have some extra time there's nothing like fresh tomatoes in the middle of summer. Just dice them and cook them for an extra 5 minutes when you add them to the dish to break them down.

Pre-Bath

Salt and pepper the shrimp, sprinkle with the cayenne pepper, then add to the sous vide pouch in a single layer. Add the butter and seal.

At this point you can store the pouch in the refrigerator for up to 2 days, freeze it for up to 6 months or cook it right away. If you freeze the pouch be sure to thaw it in the refrigerator for 1 to 2 days before cooking or increase the cooking time to compensate.

Cooking

Preheat the water bath to 122°F / 50°C for sushi quality or 132°F / 55.6°C otherwise.

Place the sous vide pouch in the water bath and cook for 15 to 35 minutes.

Finishing

Bring a pot of salted water to a boil. Heat a pan over medium to medium-high heat.

Add the linguine to the water and cook until tender.

Meanwhile, make the pomodoro sauce. Add the olive oil to the pan and heat. Cook the garlic for 1 minute then add the onion and cook until it begins to soften and turn translucent. Add the tomatoes and some of their juices to the pan and cook for 5 to 10 minutes. Whisk in the butter, add the basil and oregano, salt and pepper to taste, then mix well.

Spoon the pasta into bowls and top with the pomodoro sauce. Take the shrimp out of the pouches and place on top of the pasta. Grate the parmesan cheese on top and sprinkle with the basil and lemon zest.

FISH TACOS WITH CORN SALSA

Pre-Bath Time: 15 Minutes
Cooking Time: 10 to 30 Minutes
Finishing Time: 25 Minutes
Temperature: 122°F / 50°C for sushi quality or
132°F / 55.6°C otherwise
Serves: 4

Pre-Bath Ingredients

For the Fish
1 pound mahi mahi
2 teaspoons garlic powder
½ teaspoon paprika
¼ teaspoon chipotle powder, or chile powder of
   your choice
Salt and pepper

Finishing Ingredients

For the Corn Salsa
1 cup corn kernels, cooked
2 tomatoes, diced
1 avocado, diced
½ cup black beans, either canned or cooked
2 tablespoons chopped red onion
¼ cup fresh cilantro
4 cloves garlic, diced
2 tablespoons olive oil
1 teaspoon lime juice

For the Tacos
4-6 soft corn tortillas

*These fish tacos are inspired by some that my friend
made when I was out visiting them in Denver.
Avocado and corn always go great together and they
form the base for this flavorful salsa. If you can't find
mahi mahi you can use any flaky, white fish.*

Pre-Bath

Mix the spices together in a bowl. Salt and
pepper the mahi mahi then sprinkle with the
spices. Place in the sous vide pouches and
seal.

At this point you can store the pouch in the
refrigerator for up to 2 days, freeze it for up
to 6 months or cook it right away. If you
freeze the pouch be sure to thaw it in the
refrigerator for 1 to 2 days before cooking or
increase the cooking time to compensate.

Cooking

Preheat the water bath to 122°F / 50°C for
sushi quality or 132°F / 55.6°C otherwise.

Place the sous vide pouch in the water bath
and cook for 10 to 30 minutes.

Finishing

To make the salsa combine all of the
ingredients in a bowl and mix well.

Remove the mahi mahi from the water bath
and pat dry. Serve it with the salsa and the
corn tortillas.

SPHERIFICATION

For more tips and tricks you can visit our modernist cooking forums.
There are a lot of questions answered and information exchanged there.

You can find them on our website here:
www.modernistcookingmadeeasy.com/modernist-cooking-forums

Spherification is one of the hallmarks of modernist cooking. It is used to refer to spheres 6 mm to 30 mm / ¼" to 1" wide with a still liquid center. The smaller spheres burst like caviar when bitten and the larger ones release their liquid similar to an over easy egg yolk. When done right, if you serve these to guests who have never had them before they will be the most talked about part of the meal.

How Spherification Works

At it's most basic, spherification is controlled gelling. Some ingredients gel in any liquid, such as agar, so if it is hydrated it will set right away. However, some ingredients only gel in the presence of certain ions, such as calcium or potassium. These gelling agents are used in spherification.

You can mix the gelling agent in a flavored, neutral liquid, one lacking the ions required to gel, called a "base". If you drip this base into a "setting bath" that contains the ions, the outside of the base will begin to gel as the gelling agent interacts with the ions. If you remove it before it solidifies you will have a gel sphere, called a membrane, with a liquid center.

So using these specific ingredients in various ways allows you to control the gelling so it only occurs on the outside of the base, and only to a thickness that you prefer.

Gelling Agents, Ions, and Sequestrants

There are a few things needed to achieve spherification.

Gelling Agents

There are many gelling agents that can be used for spherification. In general, any gelling agent that requires specific ions to gel can be used. In this book we focus on using sodium alginate because it is very effective at both direct and reverse spherification. Once set, it also can be heated above the boiling point without melting, making it very versatile.

However, you can also use carrageenan, gellan, or even pectin depending on what you are gelling and the properties you want the spheres to have.

Ions

In order for the gelling agents to gel they need to be in the presence of calcium or potassium. In order to supply this you add calcium salts. There are several different ones but the most common are calcium chloride, which has a bitter taste, and calcium lactate, which we prefer to use.

Sequestrants

Some liquids you want to use in spherification might already contain calcium or potassium ions. These liquids will not work as they are because the gelling agent will gel instantly. In these cases you need to use sequestrants. Sequestrants basically tie up all the calcium and potassium ions in a liquid so they can't react with the gelling agent. You can then use the liquid for spherification like you normally would.

Some common sequestrants are sodium citrate and sodium hexametaphosphate. The full use of sequestrants is outside the scope of this book but they are usually used in a 0.1% to 0.2% ratio.

Direct vs Reverse Spherification

There are two main types of spherification, direct and reverse. At the most basic level, in direct spherification the gelling agent is in the base and in reverse spherification it is in the setting bath.

While it seems like a minor difference it causes a few changes in how they work. This is because in both methods it is always the gelling agent that gels, never the liquid containing the ions.

Gel Location

The location of the membrane is affected by the type of spherification used. In direct spherification the gelling agent is in the flavored base so the membrane grows inward as the ions reach the gelling agent. For reverse spherification the membrane grows outward, into the setting bath.

Gelling Cutoff

What happens when the spheres are removed from the setting bath is also affected by the type of spherification used. Spheres made with direct spherification will continue to gel until eventually becoming solid. This is because not only is there gelling agent in the flavored base, there is now also some ions. These ions continue to gel the liquid so the spheres must be served in a timely manner.

In reverse spherification the gelling agent is in the setting bath so once the spheres are removed there is nothing else to gel. This means these spheres can be stored for several hours before serving.

Membrane Flavor

The flavor of the membrane will depend on the type of spherification used. In direct spherification the membrane will be made of the flavored base so it will have a more pure flavor.

In reverse spherification the membrane is made up of the setting bath. Often times sugar is adding to the setting bath to make it sweeter.

Spherification Variables

There are several things to keep in mind when using spherification.

Thickness of Flavored Base

If you are not freezing the base before using it then you may want to thicken it slightly with xanthan gum. A thicker base will hold together better and keep its shape in the setting bath. Usually 0.1% to 0.4% xanthan gum will be enough to do the job.

Thickness of Setting Bath

Another variable is the thickness of the setting bath. If the flavored base is denser than the setting bath the spheres may sink to the bottom and form in non-round shapes. Thickening the setting bath to the same thickness of the flavored base will cause them to float, suspended, in the setting bath.

Acidity

Some gelling agents, like sodium alginate, do not work as well with acidic ingredients. This is more of an issue in direct spherification and is something to be aware of if you are trying to make acidic spheres.

Hot or Cold

Many gelling agents can be heated before they melt, and this means that spheres made from them can be heated as well. If you are planning on serving the spheres in a soup or on a hot dish be sure to pick a gelling agent that works well with it.

Please be careful serving spheres that are at high temperatures because they can cause severe burns since many people expect them to be cooler.

REVERSE SPHERIFICATION PROCESS

I like to start with reverse spherification because I find it much easier to do. In reverse spherification you combine a calcium salt, typically calcium lactate[14] with the flavored base you want to turn into a sphere. You then freeze this liquid in hemispherical or spherical molds, about 25 mm / 1" in diameter.

Technically, you don't have to freeze the liquid to make the spheres, it just makes the process much easier. When frozen, the spheres have no chance to break apart. It also allows you to create spheres of a uniform size more easily.

Once the base is frozen you make the setting bath. This is done by combining water with the gelling agent and sometimes some sugar. In reverse spherification I prefer using sodium alginate.

The frozen spheres of base are then placed into the bath for 1 to 5 minutes, depending on the thickness of the membrane you want. Make sure the spheres are not touching or they will fuse together.

I recommend starting with one sphere at a time to test out some different setting times. That way you can see which one works best for your specific purpose. In general I've found these times work well:

Small Spheres - 2 minutes
Medium Spheres - 4 minutes
Large Spheres - 5 minutes
Thin membrane - 1 minute
Medium Membrane - 3 minutes
Thick Membrane - 5 minutes

Once the membranes have set the spheres are removed and rinsed in a water bath. This bath can be warm or cold, depending on the temperature you would like to serve the spheres. At this point the spheres are ready to be served.

Storing the Spheres

The spheres can be stored for several hours or even overnight in liquid. However, the liquid can leech out some of the flavor so they shouldn't be left in plain water for more than 15 to 30 minutes. If you know you will be storing them for an extended period of time I recommend setting aside some of the liquid used in the base, before the calcium is added, and storing the spheres in it.

Carbonated Spheres

You can also place the finished spheres into a whipping siphon, with some reserved calcium-free liquid, charge it, and let it sit for several hours to carbonate the spheres.

Reverse Spherification Ratios

For the flavored base a ratio of 1.0% to 3.0% calcium lactate is typically used with a setting bath of 0.4-0.5% sodium alginate.

POMEGRANATE COSMO SPHERES

My wife and many of her friends enjoy cosmos, especially pomegranate cosmos. Turning the drink into spheres is a great way to add a twist to the drink while still allowing them to enjoy a favorite drink.

If you have a whipping siphon you can elevate these another level. Once the spheres have been gelled place them in the siphon, making sure to stay below the fill line. Add enough pomegranate juice to cover them and seal the siphon. Charge with one canister, and vent it out, this will clear the air out. Charge as you normally would and refrigerator for several hours before venting the siphon and serving.

This recipe will make about 30 to 50 spheres.

Tools Needed
Sodium alginate
Calcium lactate
Immersion blender
Slotted spoon
Hemispherical or spherical molds
A scale with small gram measurements

Ingredients
For the Cosmo Spheres
175 grams vodka, about ¾ cup
175 grams pomegranate juice, about ¾ cup
120 grams cointreau or triple sec, about ½ cup
60 grams fresh lime juice, about ¼ cup
10.6 grams calcium lactate, 2.0%

For the Alginate Bath
1000 grams water
65 grams sugar
5 grams sodium alginate, 0.5%

Combine the ingredients for the cosmo in a bowl using an immersion blender. Spoon the cosmo flavored base into hemispherical or spherical molds and freeze them.

Prepare the alginate bath by placing the water, sugar, and sodium alginate in a pot. Blend well with an immersion blender and bring it to a boil. Set it aside and let it cool.

Fill another bowl with water and set aside for use as the rinsing bowl.

Place the frozen cosmo spheres into the alginate bath, making sure they do not touch each other. Let them set for 2 to 4 minutes. Remove them with a slotted spoon and place them into the rinsing bath. Swirl them gently to rinse off the outsides.

They will last for about 30 minutes in the water bath, or over night in reserved pomegranate juice.

CRANBERRY SPHERES

These cranberry spheres are a great way to add some flair to a turkey dinner. I use a homemade cranberry sauce in them. It is thicker than the liquid in many spheres but it is packed with flavor. If you prefer to use a pre-made cranberry sauce you can thin it out if needed with water, orange juice, or cointreau until it is a good thickness. This recipe will make 25 to 40 spheres.

Tools Needed
Sodium alginate
Calcium lactate
Standing or immersion blender
Coarse strainer
Slotted spoon
Hemispherical or spherical molds
A scale with small gram measurements

Ingredients
For the Cranberry Sauce
170 grams cranberries, fresh or frozen, about 1 12
 -ounce package
150 grams sugar, about ½ cup
350 grams water, about 1 cup
1 cinnamon stick
60 grams cointreau or triple sec

For the Cranberry Base
400 grams cranberry sauce
8 grams calcium lactate, 2.0%

For the Alginate Bath
1000 grams water
65 grams sugar
5 grams sodium alginate, 0.5%

Combine all the ingredients for the cranberry sauce except the cointreau. Bring to a simmer at cook until the cranberries are tender and have released their juices. It should take about 20 minutes. Add the cointreau and blend well. Strain the mixture into a bowl and set aside.

Make the flavored base by combining the calcium lactate with 400 grams of the cranberry sauce in a bowl using an immersion blender. Pour the base into hemispherical or spherical molds and freeze them.

Prepare the alginate bath by placing the water, sugar, and sodium alginate in a pot. Blend well with an immersion blender and bring it to a boil. Set it aside and let it cool.

Fill another bowl with water and set aside for use as the rinsing bowl.

Place the frozen cranberry spheres into the alginate bath, making sure they do not touch each other. Let them set for 2 to 4 minutes. Remove them with a slotted spoon and place them into the rinsing bath. Swirl them gently to rinse off the outsides.

They will last for about 30 minutes in the water bath, or over night in reserved cranberry sauce. They can be served hot or cold.

DIRECT SPHERIFICATION

Making spheres with direct spherification takes more practice than with reverse spherification. Both the setting bath and the flavored base are liquid when you combine them so it takes more technique to create spheres.

One thing to keep in mind when working with direct spherification. Many bottled juices have potassium or calcium added to them and this will cause the flavored base to set before it is added to the setting bath. For these juices, and other liquids with calcium or potassium present, you will have to use a sequestrant or use use reverse spherification.

Direct Spherification Process

To make spheres with direct spherification you combine the gelling agent with the flavored base. You then prepare the setting bath by combining water with a calcium salt such as calcium chloride or calcium lactate.

To make the spheres you fill a spoon with the base and hold it just above the setting bath. Pour the base off the spoon and into the setting bath.

It should develop a membrane relatively quickly, about 1 to 3 minutes, and can then be removed. The sphere needs to be rinsed off in water to remove the setting bath from the outside.

At this point it is ready to be served. It can be held for a few minutes, about 10 to 15, depending on the size of the sphere, but it will continue to gel until it eventually becomes solid. Some people will heat the spheres near boiling to prevent further gelification from occurring.

Direct Spherification Ratios

There are several gelling agents you can use for direct spherification.

Sodium Alginate

For direct spherification a 0.5% to 1% sodium alginate base is used with a 0.5% to 1% calcium lactate setting bath.

Iota Carrageenan

For direct spherification a 1% to 3% iota carrageenan base is used with a 4% to 6% calcium lactate setting bath.

I love this simple Asian inspired sauce on a variety of meats, vegetables, and stir fries. In order to elevate it for fancy dishes I turn it into spheres that can be plated alongside, or on top of smaller bites. It's also wonderful when made as caviar instead of spheres.

Tools Needed
Sodium alginate
Calcium lactate
Immersion blender
Slotted spoon
Plastic syringe, squeeze bottle, or eye dropper
A scale with small gram measurements

Ingredients
For the Spheres
120 grams hoisin sauce, about ½ cup
60 grams rice vinegar, about ¼ cup
60 grams soy sauce, about ¼ cup
13 grams sesame oil, about 1 tablespoon
15 grams lime juice, about 1 tablespoon
13 grams honey, about 1 tablespoon
2 teaspoons ginger powder
2 teaspoons garlic powder
4 grams sodium alginate, 1.0%

For the Setting Bath
1000 grams water
10 grams calcium lactate, 1%

Add all of the ingredients for the spheres except the sodium alginate to a pot. Heat it to a simmer and remove from the heat. Add the sodium alginate and blend with an immersion blender. Let cool. For a more refined presentation you can refrigerate it for several hours or overnight so the bubbles disperse, but be sure to bring it to room temperature before making the spheres.

Make the setting bath by adding the calcium lactate to the water and blending with a clean immersion blender. Fill another bowl with water to use as the rinsing bath. Fill a third bowl with hot water to be used as the holding and bath.

Just before serving, prepare the spheres. Fill a spoon with the flavored base and hold it just above the setting bath. Pour the base off the spoon and into the setting bath. After 1 to 2 minutes take the sphere out with the slotted spoon, place it in the rinsing bath, and swirl it around gently. Remove it from the rinsing bath and place it into the holding bath. Repeat until you have used all the flavored base. You can also do several spheres at the same time.

Serve the spheres as quickly as possible because they will continue to solidify.

CAVIAR

Caviar are just small spheres. Because the spheres stick together in reverse spherification if they touch, it isn't very effective for making them. Because of this, direct spherification is usually used.

Caviar Process

The initial steps to making caviar are the same as for making larger spheres. You first make the flavored base and mix in the gelling agent. Next, you prepare the setting bath with a calcium salt.

To make the caviar, drip the base into the setting bath and let them set for 30 to 90 seconds. Remove them from the setting bath and rinse them off before serving them.

There are many ways to facilitate the dripping. You can use a plastic syringe, squeeze bottle, or eye dropper. Some people dip their finger tips in the liquid and lightly shake it off into the setting bath.

For larger quantities of caviar you can use a rapid caviar maker, which is a small box that has 50 to 100 holes that the base drips out of, greatly speeding up the process.

Caviar Ratios

The ratios for making caviar are the same for direct spherification.

Sodium Alginate

For caviar, a 0.5% to 1% sodium alginate base is used with a 0.5% to 1% calcium lactate setting bath.

Iota Carrageenan

For caviar, a 1% to 3% iota carrageenan base is used with a 4% to 6% calcium lactate setting bath.

Papaya Caviar

These small caviar provide a nice burst of flavor to a dish. The flavor of papaya is on the mild side which makes these very versatile caviar. They are a good garnish on a salad or tropical salsa. They also go well with white fish or on desserts such as ice cream.

Tools Needed
Sodium alginate
Calcium lactate
Immersion blender
Slotted spoon
Plastic syringe, squeeze bottle, or eye dropper
A scale with small gram measurements

Ingredients
For the Caviar
300 grams papaya juice
Sugar or honey, optional
3 grams sodium alginate, 1.0%

For the Setting Bath
1000 grams water
5 grams calcium lactate, 0.5%

Put the papaya juice in a bowl. Taste for sweetness and add sugar or honey if you want it sweeter. Add the sodium alginate and blend with an immersion blender. Set aside.

Make the setting bath by adding the calcium lactate to the water and blending with a clean immersion blender. Fill another bowl with water to use as the rinsing bath.

Just before serving, prepare the caviar. Slowly drip the papaya juice into the setting bath using a syringe, squeeze bottle or eye dropper. After 30-45 seconds take out the caviar with a slotted spoon, place them in the rinsing bath, and swirl them around gently. Repeat until you have used all the papaya juice.

Serve the caviar as quickly as possible because they will continue to solidify.

THICKENING

There are a wide variety of ways to thicken liquids. In Western cooking flour or another starch has traditionally been used, especially to make gravies. Reducing the liquid over heat is another common technique. Many of the modernist ingredients allow you thicken liquids more efficiently and without changing the flavor.

WHY THICKEN?

There are several reasons for thickening a liquid.

Mouthfeel

One of the biggest reason to thicken a liquid is to improve its mouthfeel. The mouthfeel is how a liquid feels on the tongue. Thickening it can add body and make it feel more rich and creamy than it typically would.

Because of the extra mouthfeel added by many thickeners it is possible to reduce the amount of fats in the dish without a reduction in richness of taste.

Cling

By thickening a liquid, and raising its viscosity, we improve how well it clings to food. This helps when applying glazes, keeping sauces on one section of the plate, or evenly coating food.

Particle Suspension

Many sauces have solid particles in them, such as herbs, spices, or purees. Thickening the liquid helps hold these solids in suspension and prevents them from sinking or floating out of the liquid.

Stabilize Emulsions

When a liquid is thickened and used in an emulsion, like a vinaigrette, it helps stabilize it for a longer time. This makes thickeners a great way to add body to an emulsion while also stabilizing it.

THICKENING PROCESS

Even though there are lots of different kinds of thickeners a similar process is used to thicken most liquids. For instructions for a specific ingredient you can see the chapter for it from the section on Ingredients.

Dispersion

The first step is to disperse the thickener in the liquid you want to thicken. Dispersion is simply the act of evenly distributing the ingredient throughout the liquid. This will ensure the liquid will be thickened uniformly instead of clumping.

Some ingredients require special dispersion methods, such as combining flour with cold water before adding it to hot water to eliminate lumps. Depending on the ingredient, you may have to use a hot, cold, acidic, or other liquid for proper dispersion. For some ingredients a whisk or spoon will work fine, others will need the stronger shearing forces of an immersion or standing blender.

Hydration

Once the thickener has been fully dispersed it needs to hydrate. Hydration is basically the process of absorbing water, or another liquid, and swelling. This absorption of liquid, in conjunction with other processes, causes the thickening of the mixture, creating a molecular mesh that traps water.

Depending on the thickener and the liquid being used, hydration will occur at different temperatures and over different time frames. Many ingredients will need to be heated for hydration to occur, like flour and carrageenan, and some will hydrate at any temperature, such as xanthan gum.

Setting

The final stage is when the liquid actually thickens. Many thickeners will only begin to work below a specific temperature, while others will work at any temperature. This process typically takes only a few minutes.

COMMON THICKENERS

There are many different thickeners and we cover four of them in-depth in this book.

For an extended look at any of these ingredients please see their entry in the Ingredients section. We also touch on a few others in the Other Ingredients section.

Carrageenan

There are many types of carrageenan and they are very good at thickening dairy products and adding good mouthfeel. The liquid has to be heated before the carrageenan will hydrate.

Mono and Diglycerides

Mono and diglycerides are used to thicken and emulsify oils and fats. They are introduced by heating the oil and dissolving them into it.

Tapioca Maltodextrin

Commonly called N-Zorbit M or Texturas Malto, tapioca maltodextrin thickens oils. This can range from creating a light paste to a fine powder. It is commonly stirred or whisked into the oil until the desired texture is achieved.

Xanthan Gum

A good all around thickener that hydrates at almost any temperature and a wide range of pH. It is commonly used at ratios of 0.2% to 1%, though it can result in an undesirable mouthfeel at high concentrations, almost resembling mucus. Because it hydrates and thickens very quickly it can be added slowly to a liquid until it obtains the thickness desired, removing the need to always weigh it.

CHIMICHURRI SAUCE

Chimichurri is a very flavorful Argentinian sauce that is used both to marinate and sauce dishes. There are many different varieties and here is one of my favorites.

Chimichurri is usually made with culantro, but that can be very hard to find so here I substitute cilantro, which has a similar flavor. You can also use parsley if you prefer.

The small amount of xanthan gum helps to thicken the sauce slightly and prevent it from breaking, as well as more effectively suspending the herbs. It can be used on grilled steak like a traditional chimichurri but it is also great on chicken or a topping for vegetables.

Tools Needed
Xanthan gum
Standing or immersion blender
A scale with small gram measurements

Ingredients
1 bunch culantro or cilantro
6 garlic cloves, coarsely chopped
3 tablespoons onion, diced
73 grams cider vinegar, about 5 tablespoons
60 grams water, about 4 tablespoons
2 teaspoons dried oregano
1 teaspoon hot pepper flakes, or to taste
Salt and pepper
215 grams olive oil, about 1 cup
0.7 grams xanthan gum, 0.2%

Add all of the ingredients except the xanthan gum to a blender or a container that works well with your immersion blender. Blend well to combine the ingredients.

Taste the sauce for seasoning and adjust the olive oil and vinegar to control the acidity. Once the sauce tastes balanced, sprinkle in the xanthan gum and blend well to combine.

Bourbon Glaze

This bourbon glaze is one of my most raved about recipes. It's often used as a glaze on grilled pork or chicken but can also be used as a sauce after the food has been cooked.

Traditionally, the sauce would need to be simmer for 30 minutes in order to reduce it to a good consistency. The addition of the xanthan gum cuts the whole cooking time to under 10 minutes from start to finish.

Tools Needed

Xanthan gum
Immersion blender
A scale with small gram measurements

Ingredients

207 grams bourbon whiskey, about 1 cup
110 grams brown sugar, about ½ cup
140 grams ketchup, about ½ cup
10 grams Worcester sauce, about 2 teaspoons
5 grams liquid smoke, about 1 teaspoon
60 grams apple juice, about ¼ cup
12 grams lemon juice, about 1 tablespoon
1 teaspoon chopped garlic
½ teaspoon cayenne pepper
¼ teaspoon dry mustard
Salt and pepper
1.5 grams xanthan gum, 0.3%

Add all of the ingredients except the xanthan gum to a pot over medium-high heat. Bring to a simmer, stirring occasionally.

Taste the glaze for seasoning and adjust as needed. Once the glaze tastes balanced, remove from the heat.

Sprinkle in some of the xanthan gum and blend well to combine. Taste it for thickness and mouthfeel. If you need it thicker, continue adding xanthan gum and blending well until it has the thickness and mouthfeel you are looking for.

Apple Cider Syrup

The combination of apples and pork goes way back. When I cook pork chops I like to make a pan sauce using apple cider and then reduce it to a thick syrup. However, sometimes I'm in a rush and want something to come together quickly so I'll make this version of the sauce. It's not quite as complex and nuanced but it's much quicker to put together and uses about a quarter as much butter. It also has a much brighter flavor because the cider hasn't caramelized while it was reducing.

Tools Needed
Xanthan gum
Immersion blender
A scale with small gram measurements

Ingredients
1 tablespoon butter
1 shallot, minced
2 tablespoons chopped sage leaves
Salt and pepper
350 grams good apple cider, about 1½ cups
1.75 grams xanthan gum, 0.5%

Melt the butter in a small pot over medium heat. Add the shallot, sage, salt, and pepper then cook for 5 minutes.

Add the apple cider and let come up to temperature. Sprinkle the xanthan gum in the cider and blend will with an immersion blender.

Remove from the heat and spoon on pork or another food.

LOW FAT CHOCOLATE MILK SHAKE

In this recipe I use xanthan gum to thicken milk to emulate a chocolate milk shake. There are several advantages to this method over using ice cream to create a milk shake. You can use skim milk in this recipe and the taste does not change much, so you can have a very low fat milk shake. The milk shake also will not "melt" like a real milk shake would.

It might not replace a thick, homestyle milkshake but it can be a much healthy snack!

Tools Needed
Xanthan gum
Standing blender
A scale with small gram measurements

Ingredients
25 grams sugar, about 2 tablespoons
500 grams milk, about 2 cups
1 banana
A few drops vanilla extract, to taste
10 grams cocoa powder, about 2 teaspoons
½ teaspoon ground cinnamon
12 ice cubes
2 grams xanthan gum, 0.4%

Add all of the ingredients except the xanthan gum to a blender. Blend well until it becomes a smooth mixture.

Turn the blender to a speed that forms a vortex. Sprinkle the xanthan gum into the blender and mix well.

The milk shake is now ready to drink.

CINNAMON PUDDING

There are many ways to make pudding but I like this version using iota carrageenan. It uses much less thickener than a traditional pudding, making the flavors stand out more. You also use milk instead of cream without sacrificing mouthfeel.

This is my quick version of the recipe. If you want a more refined version steep the milk with some cinnamon sticks and a vanilla bean instead of using the extract. The pudding should either be set in the serving dishes, it is too fragile to unmold, or pureed after setting for a finer texture and poured into a serving dish.

Tools Needed
Iota carrageenan
Immersion blender
Molds
A scale with small gram measurements

Ingredients
500 grams milk, preferably 2% or whole, about 2 cups
0.2 grams iota carrageenan, 0.04%
1 tablespoon powdered cinnamon
½ teaspoon vanilla extract
16 grams white sugar, about 2 teaspoons

Place 250 grams of the milk in a pot. Mix in the iota carrageenan with an immersion blender until combined well. Bring the milk to a simmer over medium to medium-high heat and blend again for 30 to 60 seconds with the immersion blender to ensure even distribution and full hydration.

Stir in the cinnamon, vanilla, and sugar and blend for 30 seconds with the immersion blender until fully combined. Taste and adjust the flavors as needed, they will be diluted with the additional milk but you should be able to balance them at this point.

Remove the pot from the heat and blend in the remaining milk with the immersion blender.

Place the pudding in the refrigerator to set. Once it has cooled and set you can serve as is or use the immersion blender to briefly break it up into a creamier pudding.

This bacon powder is a great way to add flavor and texture to different dishes. I've used it to sprinkle over New England clam chowder at the last minute to add a visual treat and a flavor that melts through the dish. I've also used the more paste-like version as a spread on BLTs and lox. You can follow this general recipe with almost any type of oil.

Tools Needed
Tapioca maltodextrin
A scale with small gram measurements

Ingredients
100 grams rendered bacon fat
3 grams salt
50 - 80 grams tapioca maltodextrin, the actual amount will depend on the quality and type of bacon fat you use, 50% - 80%

Heat the rendered bacon fat until it becomes a liquid. Pour it into a bowl large enough to comfortably hold it. Whisk in the salt.

To turn the bacon fat into powder begin to whisk in the tapioca maltodextrin. Once it begins to thicken and clump you can add it in more slowly and you may have to start using a fork to incorporate the maltodextrin as whisks will often fill with the paste. Continue to add tapioca maltodextrin while mixing until it forms the texture you want.

For a finer, more powder-like texture you can run the thickened bacon fat through a tamis or, to a lesser extent, a chinois.

When you are ready to serve the bacon powder simply spoon or sprinkle it over the dish.

The powder will last for several hours at room temperature or in the refrigerator for several days.

JALAPENO SPREAD

This jalapeno spread infuses the heat of jalapenos into canola oil which is then thickened. It is a good topping to grilled meats, or a spicy spread for bread. This process of infusing oil with flavors before thickening it leads to countless variations you can adapt to any dish.

Tools Needed
Mono and Diglyceride (Glycerin) Flakes
Whisk
Chinois or strainer
Standing or immersion blender, optional
A scale with small gram measurements

Ingredients
215 grams olive oil, about 1 cup
1-2 jalapeno peppers, cut into rings
¼ onion, sliced
Salt and pepper
16 grams mono and diglyceride (glycerin) flakes, 7.5%

Combine the olive oil, jalapeno peppers, and onion in a pan set over medium heat. Salt and pepper them. Heat for 5 to 10 minutes, until the peppers and onions soften.

If you want a more flavorful oil you can puree with a blender.

Strain the olive oil to remove the solids. Return the oil to the pot and stir in the glycerin flakes until they have melted then remove the pot from the heat. Let come to room temperature then refrigerate for several hours.

Once cold, and you are ready to use, whisk the oil until it forms the consistency of mayonnaise.

ROASTED GARLIC OLIVE OIL SPREAD

This roasted garlic olive oil is a great way to change up the textures of a dish without changing the flavors. The spread is simply garlic infused olive oil that has been thickened with mono and diglyceride flakes. This thickened oil can then be whipped into a spread and used as a sauce or spread on a variety of dishes.

This technique can be used on most oils and can result in a wide range of flavors. Infusing the oil with different flavors before thickening them adds a lot of variety.

Tools Needed
Mono and Diglyceride (Glycerin) Flakes
Whisk
A scale with small gram measurements

Ingredients
215 grams olive oil, about 1 cup
7 cloves garlic, roughly chopped
16 grams mono and diglyceride (glycerin) flakes, 7.5%

Combine the garlic and olive oil in a pan set over medium heat. Heat just until the garlic starts to sizzle. Let steep for 5 to 10 minutes, making sure the garlic does not burn.

Stir in the glycerin flakes until they have melted. Remove from the heat and strain into a mixing bowl. Let it come to room temperature then refrigerate for several hours.

Once cold, whisk the oil until it forms the consistency of mayonnaise.

OTHER TECHNIQUES

We are always adding new techniques to our website. You can follow all the latest techniques we are exploring.

You can find them on our website at:
www.modernistcookingmadeeasy.com/info/modernist-techniques

We tried to focus on the previous techniques because we think they are the most accessible to the home cook or chef on a budget. Because of this we had to overlook several techniques, including some more advanced techniques that require more expensive equipment or expertise with handling semi-dangerous chemical.

These techniques are still important and worth keeping an eye on. Here are some summaries of them.

CENTRIFUGAL SEPARATION

Centrifuges have been used in labs to separate liquids into their component parts, such as removing platelets from blood. Cooks can use the same process to break cooking liquids into their component parts. This can be used to clarify stocks or juices and is probably the best way to strain solids out of a liquid.

COMPRESSION

There are several ways to compress foods but the most commonly used these days is chambered vacuum sealers. They can be used to increase the density of foods like watermelon, changing their texture flavor.

DEHYDRATION

Dehydration is one of the techniques that is accessible to home cooks and chefs because it can be done in the oven or with an inexpensive dehydrator. It has many uses including making beef jerky, fruit leathers, or dried fruits. It can also be used to set foams, such as meringues, or to dry out gels to create flexible or crispy sheets.

FREEZE DRYING

Freeze drying has been around industrial food production for several decades and it is slowly moving into restaurant kitchens. Freeze drying basically freezes food while also removing the moisture from it.

FREEZING

Freezing has been used in cooking for a long time, both to preserve food and to create new foods. While the old freezing methods are still used there are a few new ways of freezing that are taking precedence in many professional kitchens.

Anti-Griddle

The anti-griddle looks like a box with a griddle on top of it but instead of being very hot it is very cold. Liquids or purees on it freeze almost instantly allowing you to create unique shapes or to just freeze the outside, leaving the inside liquid.

Liquid Nitrogen

Liquid nitrogen is also being explored in the kitchen. Its ability to instantly freeze anything that come into contact with it opens up many doors for chefs. It can be used to create solids and brittles from sauces and liquids, as well as freeze liquids into interesting shapes.

ROTARY EVAPORATION

Rotary evaporators use a combination of heat, vacuum, and rotation to create extracts and essential oils of foods. Similar to vanilla extract[15], these extracts can be taken from a wide variety of foods and used for intense flavors.

SECTION THREE

MODERNIST COOKING INGREDIENTS

AGAR

Have a "How To" question about modernist cooking? Check out our "How To" page to see if it is answered, or submit it and we might answer it for you!

You can find them on our website at:
www.modernistcookingmadeeasy.com/info/how-to

Common Names
Agar, Agar Agar, Agazoon

Basic Ratios By Weight
0.2% soft gels
0.5-3% firm gels
0.5-2% fluid gels when blended
0.3-1% light foams
1-2% dense foams

Dispersion Temperature
Any

Hydration Temperature
100°C / 212°F for 3 to 5 minutes

Setting Temperature
40-45°C / 104-113°F

Melting Temperature
80°C / 175°F

Agar, or agar agar, is an extract from red algae that is often used to stabilize emulsions or foams and to thicken or gel liquids. While many people in America have only heard of it lately it has been used for hundreds of years in Asian cooking.

Agar is also relatively straightforward to work with and easy to find online, making it a great place to start experimenting with modernist cooking.

DISPERSION AND HYDRATION

In order for agar to be used effectively it has to be properly dispersed and hydrated.

Dispersing the Agar

Unlike many ingredients, you can add agar to hot or cold liquids. It can typically be mixed in using a whisk, though an immersion or standing blender works more efficiently.

Hydrating the Agar

In order for agar to work effectively it first needs to hydrate, or absorb water. To hydrate, agar needs to be brought to a boil at 100°C / 212°F and simmered for 3 to 5 minutes.

Agar does not hydrate well in acidic liquids, less than a 5 ph, and should be hydrated first before acidic components are added to the mixture.

AGAR GELS

Agar is commonly used to create gels of different strengths. It can range from very soft gels to firm jellies, depending on the other ingredients and the amount of agar used.

When used by itself to gel a liquid, agar results in a rigid, brittle gel. This means that it will break down quickly on cutting or biting. To make a chewier, elastic gel, you can add locust bean gum or other ingredients to the agar.

A nice property of agar gels is that they can be used hot or cold. They will not melt until they go above 80°C / 176°F which allows you to use them in soups or other hot foods. They can also be melted and re-set multiple times without a loss in strength.

Adding sugar to agar gels results in a shiner gel. Agar also works well for gelling alcohol. However, you cannot freeze agar gels, since freezing causes a loss in liquid and texture, unless you are trying to clarify liquids through the freeze thaw technique[16].

Agar Gelling Ratios

The amount of agar you will use depends on how firm of a gel you would like to create. In general, you will use a 0.2% ratio for a soft gel, 0.5% for a more firm gel, and up to 3% for the firmest gels. Fluid gels are typically made from a 0.5% to 2% ratio agar gel, with thicker fluid gels using a higher percent.

Agar Gelling Process

To make an agar gel you combine the agar with the liquid you would like to gel. Bring the mixture to a boil, then pour the agar into molds. It will begin to set very quickly once the temperature drops below 45°C / 113°F and the gelling should be completed in a matter of hours for most mold sizes, and within minutes for smaller molds.

Once it has set, the gel can be turned out, shaped, and plated. The gel will maintain its form as long as it stays below 80°C / 176°F. Please be careful serving gels that are at such a high temperature since they can

cause severe burns because many people expect them to be cool.

The gel will also last for a day or two, though it starts to lose some of its texture and moisture as it dries out over time through syneresis, the leaking of liquid from a gel. You can usually rehydrate the gels by placing them in water.

Gelling Raw Ingredients

Sometimes you do not want to bring the liquid you are gelling to a boil. In order to hydrate the agar you have two options.

You can disperse and hydrate the agar in a small amount of the liquid and blend the rest of the liquid into it after hydration. You can also disperse and hydrate the agar in water and blend the liquid into that. Either way, the temperature will drop quickly and the gel will start to set as soon as it gets below 45°C / 113°F so warming up the liquid as much as you can is advised for better dispersion once the agar has hydrated.

Hysteresis

One of the more interesting features of agar gels is the difference between their setting and melting points, referred to as hysteresis.

Most substances have specific points where they change phase. For example, water is ice below 0°C / 32°F, steam above 100°C / 212°F, and liquid in between[17].

On the other hand, agar mixtures are a gel below 45°C / 113°F and a liquid above 80°C / 176°F. But between those temperatures agar can be a liquid or a gel, and it will stay in whichever phase it is currently in. So once you cool the gel and it sets, you can reheat it above the setting point without it melting.

Synergies
Agar works well when used with many other ingredients.

Locust bean gum has several uses with agar. It helps prevent syneresis when added in small amounts, about 0.2%.

It also works with agar to create a more elastic gel if you add it as 5% to 15% of the weight of the agar. Ideas in Food suggest using a 9:1 ratio for best results[18].

The strength of agar gels can be increased by the addition of xanthan gum, methylcellulose, and guar gum, among others. Agar and gelatin also combine well to create a range of gels. Some of these synergies are covered in recipes in this book.

Papaya Cubes

These agar gel cubes are a great way to add a unique visual style to a dish, as well as create little bursts of papaya. You could use a similar agar recipe to gel many different liquids, depending on the dish you are creating and what flavors you want to complement it. Fresh juices are always ideal but if you are in a pinch Goya sells many different canned juices.

Tools Needed
Agar
Whisk or immersion blender
A scale with small gram measurements
Small flat bottom mold or container
Chinois, optional

Ingredients
200 grams papaya juice
3 grams agar, 1.5%

First prepare your mold by lining a flat-bottomed mold or container with parchment paper or spray with cooking spray. The container should be a depth that is equal to how tall you want the cubes to be.

Bring the papaya juices to a simmer in a pan. Add the agar and mix well, preferably with an immersion blender. Let simmer for 3 to 5 minutes.

If using non-strained juice then you can strain the mixture through a chinois for a clearer gel.

Pour the liquid into the parchment paper lined mold. Place the liquid in the refrigerator for quick setting. You can also leave it on the counter for slightly slower setting as long as it is below 35°C / 95°F.

Once the gel has cooled and become firm turn it out onto a cutting board. Cut the papaya agar gel into the shapes you desire using a knife or other cutting device.

Hold covered in the refrigerator or at room temperature until ready to serve. The cubes will remain a gel as long as they stay below 80°C / 176°F.

BLOODY MARYS ON A LOG

My wife's relatives in Florida love their Bloody Marys and this is her modernist take on them, focusing on the celery garnish and turning it into the serving vessel a la the traditional "ants on a log" children's snack.

I made a custom Bloody Mary mix using fresh tomatoes from the garden blended with some string beans, cayenne chile powder, ancho chile powder, and lemon juice. This mix also works great as a quick chilled tomato soup. You can also use your favorite store-bought Bloody Mary mix if you don't want to make your own version.

I added the vodka at about a 1 to 4 ratio with the Bloody Mary mix but you can change the amount to suit your taste. Just be sure to weigh the liquid at the end and adjust the agar to be 1% of that weight.

The directions to make the Bloody Mary gel also work well to gel tomato soups or other tomato sauces.

Makes 40 to 60 bites

Tools Needed
Agar
Whisk or immersion blender
A scale with small gram measurements
Food processor

Ingredients
For the Bloody Mary Gel
250 grams Bloody Mary mix
60 grams vodka
3.25 grams agar, 1%

For the Crumbled Bacon
6-8 bacon strips

For the Garnish
Fennel fronds
15-30 green olives, sliced
5 to 10 celery stalks

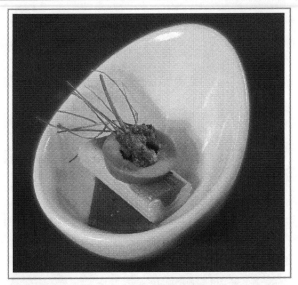

For the Crumbled Bacon
Cook the bacon strips until all the fat is rendered and they are extra crispy. I tend to bake them in a 176°C / 350°F oven on a rack set over a sheet pan until crisp, about 20 to 30 minutes.

Pat off as much oil as possible with a paper towel and let cool. For extra-crumbly bacon you can put the cooked strips in a dehydrator for a few hours.

Place the strips into a food processor and process until it becomes a chunky, crumbly paste.

Set aside until ready to use. It will last at room temperature for an hour or two or in the refrigerator for a day or two.

Note: You can also reserve the rendered bacon fat to make bacon powder for other dishes.

Prepare the Celery

Place the celery stalks on a parchment paper-lined sheet pan or other flat tray.

Make sure the celery stalks are sitting so they can hold the liquid, you may need to cut the bottom ⅛" off the stalk so they sit flat.

For the Bloody Mary Gel

Combine the Bloody Mary mix, vodka, and agar in a pot and whisk or blend together. Bring to a boil while whisking occasionally. Let simmer for 3 minutes to ensure the agar is fully hydrated.

At this stage the agar gel will set very quickly once it cools below 45°C / 113°F. I recommend keeping the pan on the burner, turned down, to keep the gel from setting as you work on filling the celery.

Spoon or pipe the hot Bloody Mary mix into the prepared celery stalks. Some will probably spill out on the sides or ends, which is fine and you can easily clean up the stalks once the agar sets.

Wait about 2 minutes, until the first mix has set, and then add another layer on top of it.

Repeat until the celery is full of Bloody Mary mix.

Pour the remaining Bloody Mary mix into a flat bottomed container to a depth of about ½" to 1" / 12 to 24mm.

Let the celery and the block of gel sit until they have set and then cover with cling wrap and store in the refrigerator until you are ready to plate, up to 24 hours.

Plating the Dish

Clean the Bloody Mary gel off the sides of the celery so they look nice and clean. Cut the stalks into 1" / 24mm pieces.

Remove the block of Bloody Mary gel from the container and slice into ⅛" / 3mm strips. Cut the strips into the same length as the celery pieces.

Place a strip of the Bloody Mary gel onto a plate or serving container. Top with a piece of the celery, turned 90° from the gel. Place a slice of olive on top of the celery and fill with bacon crumbles. Add a fennel frond or two and serve.

Ingredients: Agar 120

AGAR FLUID GELS

Fluid gels[19] are substances that behave like a gel when at rest and like a liquid when force is applied. Ketchup is probably the best know example of a fluid gel, as anyone that has struggled to get it out of the bottle, only to have it flood their hamburger, can attest.

Agar Fluid Gel Process

To create an agar fluid gel you first make a normal agar gel and let it set fully. Once it is set you blend or puree it until it is smooth.

One thing to keep in mind when creating fluid gels is that you need enough gel to easily blend. For instance, it is very hard to make 1 cup of fluid gel because the blender will just throw the gel on the walls of the blender and not puree it. It's much easier to make 2 or 3 cups and reserve the rest for a later use. For smaller amounts using an immersion blender can be helpful.

Agar Fluid Gel Ratios

The strength of the gel will determine the final viscosity of the fluid gel which can range from very thick to relatively thin. The fluid gel can also be thickened with a small amount of xanthan gum or thinned out by blending in a liquid.

Typically a ratio of 0.5% to 2% will result in a fluid gel ranging from runny to pudding like.

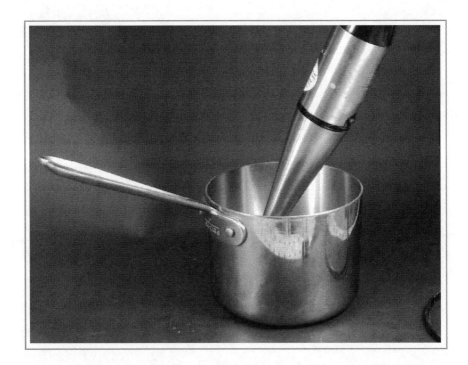

TOMATILLO PUDDING

This tomatillo fluid gel has almost a pudding like consistency. It is a great topping for sliced skirt steak or chicken breast. I also use it as a sauce for hors d'oeuvres, like the salmon cracker shown above.

I give recommendations for the amount of honey to add but tomatillos can vary greatly in their sweetness so you might need more or less. You can also use an immersion blender for the initial pureeing of the tomatillos but it will be a little less smooth of a puree.

Tools Needed
Agar
Standing or immersion blender
A scale with small gram measurements

Ingredients
400 grams tomatillos, dehusked, washed, and
    stem removed
42 grams honey, about 2 tablespoons
Salt and pepper
4 grams agar, 1.0%
0.4-1.6 grams xanthan gum, optional, 0.1% - 0.4%

Place the tomatillos in the standing blender and add the honey. Puree until smooth. Salt and pepper to taste.

Add the agar and blend until combined.

Pour the tomatillo puree into a sauce pan and bring to a boil. Let simmer for 3 to 5 minutes. Pour the tomatillo puree into a container and let it completely set.

Once it is set, cube the gel. Puree the tomatillo gel using a blender, immersion blender, or food processor until smooth. Add some water if you need to thin it, or some xanthan gum to thicken it.

Once it reaches the desired consistency it is ready to be served.

Agar Foams

Agar can also be used to make various types of foams ranging from light, coarse foams to thick, fine foams. Agar foams are usually made with a whipping siphon for easy aeration.

Agar foams can be either hot or cold. You can add other ingredients such as xanthan gum, gelatin, and locust bean gum, to help control the density of the foam.

Agar Foaming Process

Making agar foams builds on the process of making agar gels and fluid gels. You first make an agar gel, puree it into a fluid gel, and then place it into the whipping siphon.

Agar Foaming Ratios

The more agar you use the denser the resulting foam will be. For light foams, a ratio of 0.3% to 1% works well. For denser foams 1% to 2% is recommended. You can also add gelatin, locust bean gum, or xanthan gum, to change the density of the foam.

Hot Lobster Bisque Foam

I first had a similar foam to this at Seasonal, a restaurant in New York City that serves modern Austrian food. They used it as a topping for poached lobster and a soft boiled egg. The foam adds a great base of flavor to the whole dish.

Since my wife loves lobster I decided to try and recreate it at home. Sometimes I will make my own lobster stock but often times I will just buy some from my local fish market. Any smooth lobster bisque will work but I aim for a thinner bisque for finer bubbles. Depending on the thickness of the bisque you may need to use more or less agar. You can also add some xanthan gum to thicken the fluid gel if you need.

Tools Needed
Agar
Xanthan gum, optional
Standing or immersion blender
Whipping siphon
A scale with small gram measurements

Ingredients
500 grams fresh lobster stock
2.5 grams agar, 0.5%
0.5-2 grams xanthan gum, optional, 0.1% - 0.4%

Blend the lobster stock and agar together.

Pour the lobster stock into a sauce pan and bring to a boil. Let simmer for 3 to 5 minutes then pour into a container and let it completely set.

Once it is set, cube the gel and puree with a blender until smooth. Add some water if you need to thin it, or some xanthan gum to thicken it.

Pour the fluid gel into your whipping siphon and charge. Heat the whipper in hot water until it is warm, I tend to use water between 55°C / 131°F to 60.5°C / 141°F because that is what my sous vide machine is running at but any water below 80°C / 175°F should be fine.

Once the bisque has come up to temperature you can dispense it onto your dishes.

CARRAGEENAN

We are constantly adding recipes to our website as we continue to experiment with modernist cooking. Maybe something there will inspire you.

You can find them at:
www.modernistcookingmadeeasy.com/info/modernist-recipes

Carrageenan is a natural extract from red seaweed. Carrageenan has been used for hundreds of years in Ireland and Europe to turn milk into pudding.

When carrageenan is processed, it is sorted into three different kinds: iota, kappa, and lambda. Each type of carrageenan has unique properties. The three types can also be combined with each other to create a variety of textures in gels.

Iota and kappa are the most commonly used and we will look at them in depth.

Carrageenan works very well with dairy products. The carrageenan reacts with the proteins in the dairy and is much more efficient in dairy products.

DISPERSION AND HYDRATION

Both iota and kappa carrageenan are dispersed and hydrated in a similar way.

Dispersion

Iota and kappa carrageenan are best dispersed in cool liquids. This will prevent hydration until the liquid is heated. A standing or immersion blender is the preferred tool to disperse the carrageenan.

Hydration

Iota and kappa carrageenan both become hydrated above 70°C / 158°F so the liquid will have to be heated.

IOTA CARRAGEENAN

Iota carrageenan can be used to thicken liquids, stabilize emulsions or foams, and create gels. It is often used with dairy products because it reacts with the calcium in the dairy and is much more effective. The calcium also can be used to create elastic gels.

Iota carrageenan does not hydrate well with sugar and so sugar should be added after the hydration process is completed.

IOTA CARRAGEENAN THICKENING

The simplest application of iota carrageenan is the thickening of dairy products. Adding iota carrageenan to dairy based drinks is a great way to add thickness and improve mouthfeel.

Iota Carrageenan Thickening Process

To thicken a dairy-based liquid first disperse the iota carrageenan into the liquid when it is cold. Next, heat the liquid above 70°C / 158°F to hydrate the iota carrageenan. Let the liquid cool and it will become thicker.

Iota Carrageenan Gel Ratios

The amount of thickening that will occur depends on how much iota carrageenan you add. Typically a ratio of 0.02% to 0.04% will result in a good amount of thickening.

I love a good chocolate milk, especially when it has some added heat from chipotle peppers. It's very easy to make and can last in the fridge for several days if you want to make a larger quantity.

I've given my preferences for chocolate milk in the recipe but feel free to adjust the amounts of sugar, cocoa powder, and hot sauce to your own tastes. You can also make this a low-fat recipe by using skim milk and increasing the amount of iota carrageenan to 0.15. Substituting honey or agave syrup is also a good way to subtly change the flavors.

Tools Needed
Iota carrageenan
Immersion blender
A scale with small gram measurements

Ingredients
500 grams milk, preferably 2% or whole, about 2 cups
0.1 grams iota carrageenan, 0.02%
10 grams cocoa powder, about 2 teaspoons
1-4 drops chipotle hot sauce, to taste
16 grams white sugar, about 2 teaspoons

Place 250 grams of the milk in a pot. Mix in the iota carrageenan with an immersion blender until combined well. Bring the milk to a simmer over medium to medium-high heat and blend again for 30 to 60 seconds with the immersion blender to ensure even distribution and full hydration.

Stir in the cocoa powder, hot sauce, and sugar and blend for 30 seconds with the immersion blender until fully combined. Taste and adjust the chocolate, sugar, and chipotle levels as needed, they will be diluted with the additional milk but you should be able to balance them at this point.

Remove the pot from the heat and blend in the remaining milk with the immersion blender.

Put the milk in the refrigerator to chill completely. It can then be drunk as is or stored in the refrigerator for several days. It may need a quick blend with the immersion blender if it has set.

Iota Carrageenan Gels

One of the areas that iota carrageenan excels is in the creation of gels. These gels can range from the consistency of soft custard to firm custard. They are typically elastic, but they can become more brittle when mixed with other ingredients, especially kappa carrageenan.

To gel, the liquid must contain calcium that is free to bind with the iota carrageenan. If the base ingredient lacks calcium it can be added in the form of calcium salts like calcium lactate or calcium chloride.

Iota Carrageenan Gel Process

To make a gel you combine the iota carrageenan with the liquid you would like to gel. Bring the mixture above 70°C / 158°F and as high as a boil, then pour the liquid into molds. It will begin to set around 40-70°C / 104-158°F, depending on the calcium and ion content of the liquid. Let cool to room temperature, or in an ice bath, and then place in the refrigerator to finish setting. It should be fully set after a few hours for most mold sizes.

Once it has set, the gel can be turned out, shaped, and plated. The gel will maintain its form as long as it stays cooler than 5-10°C / 9-18°F above its setting temperature. Please be careful serving gels that are at such a high temperature. They can cause severe burns because many people expect them to be cool.

The gel will also last for a day or two in the refrigerator.

Iota Carrageenan Gel Ratios

The amount of iota carrageenan you use is dependent on the type of liquid you are gelling, and the firmness of the gel you are trying to create. For typical dairy gels you can use a 0.4% to 1.5% ratio. For non-dairy gels, a 0.75% to 1.5% is pretty standard.

Poblano Custard

This creamy custard is full of poblano flavor and great as an additional to many different dishes. You can serve it alongside pork chops or pork belly, or even as a side with fish.

For additional flavor you can roast the poblano peppers and the garlic. Feel free to tweak the amount of peppers, garlic, and spices to meet your own tastes and how you plan to serve it. You can also use other peppers and spices to really tailor it to the dishes you are making.

Tools Needed
Iota carrageenan
Immersion blender
Molds or setting containers
Chinois
A scale with small gram measurements

Ingredients
1 teaspoon whole coriander
1 teaspoon whole peppercorns
½ teaspoon whole cumin
½ teaspoon whole cloves
500 grams milk, about 2 cups
1-2 poblano peppers, roughly diced
4 garlic cloves, roughly diced
Salt and pepper
5 grams iota carrageenan, 1%

Place a small pan over medium heat. Add the coriander, peppercorns, cumin, and cloves and toast until fragrant, just a few minutes.

Pour the milk into a pot and add the spices, peppers, and garlic. Heat over medium-high heat, stirring occasionally to prevent scorching, and bring to a boil. Once it boils, blend with an immersion blender until slightly pureed. Remove from the heat and let steep for 20 to 30 minutes. Salt and pepper to taste.

Strain the milk, preferably through a chinois for the finest texture. Return the milk to the pot and add the iota carrageenan and blend well with an immersion blender. Bring to a boil and blend for 30 to 60 seconds. Remove from the heat and pour into molds.

Let cool at room temperature, or in an ice bath, then place in the refrigerator to finish setting.

Once fully set the gel can be turned out and cut into any shapes desired. The gel should last for several days covered in the refrigerator.

IOTA CARRAGEENAN FLUID GELS

As with many gelling agents, fluid gels can be easily made from iota carrageenan gels by blending or pureeing them.

Iota Carrageenan Fluid Gel Process

To create an iota carrageenan fluid gel you first make a normal iota carrageenan gel and let it set fully. Once it is set you blend or puree it until it is smooth.

One thing to keep in mind when creating fluid gels is that you need enough gel to easily blend. For instance, it is very hard to make 1 cup of fluid gel because the blender will just throw the gel on the walls of the blender and not puree it. It's much easier to make 2 or 3 cups and reserve the rest for a later use. For smaller amounts using an immersion blender can be helpful.

Iota Carrageenan Fluid Gel Ratios

The strength of the gel will determine the final viscosity of the fluid gel which can range from very thick to relatively thin. The fluid gel can also be thickened with a small amount of xanthan gum or thinned out by blending in a liquid.

Typically a ratio of 0.1% to 1% will result in a fluid gel ranging from a thin cream sauce to pudding like.

GARLIC CREAM SAUCE

Making a cream sauce can sometimes be a hassle, especially trying to reduce it to get the thickness you want. Using iota carrageenan makes the thickening process very easy to consistently replicate. The roasted garlic adds great flavor to the richness of the cream.

The cream is great as a finishing sauce on many dishes, including steaks and meatier fish. It is also a good way to add flavor to vegetables like asparagus or broccoli. I love using it with biscuits and gravy as well.

Because of the thickness provided from the iota carrageenan, you can even get away with using 2% milk in this recipe and the result will still have a nice, creamy texture.

Tools Needed
Iota Carrageenan
Standing or immersion blender
Chinois
A scale with small gram measurements

Ingredients
1 large head garlic
500 grams heavy cream, about 2 cups
1 sprig of rosemary
Salt and pepper
1 gram iota carrageenan, 0.2%
0.5-2 grams xanthan gum, optional, 0.1% - 0.4%

Preheat an oven or toaster oven to 200°C / 400°F.

Cut the end off the garlic, exposing one end of the cloves and drizzle with olive oil. Wrap the garlic in aluminum foil. Cook in the oven for 30 to 40 minutes, until the cloves are soft. Let cool enough so you can comfortably handle them.

Pour the cream into a pot, add the rosemary, and squeeze in as much garlic as you can. If some of the paper gets in that is fine because you will strain it at the end. Bring to a simmer while stirring occasionally and puree with an immersion blender until slightly pureed. Remove from the heat and let steep for 20 to 30 minutes. Salt and pepper to taste.

Strain the milk, preferably through a chinois for the finest texture. Return the milk to the pot and add the iota carrageenan and blend well with an immersion blender. Bring to a simmer and blend for 30 to 60 seconds. Remove from the heat and pour into a container for it to set.

Let cool at room temperature, or in an ice bath, then place in the refrigerator to finish setting.

Once fully set cut the gel into cubes and puree with a standing or immersion blender, or food processor until nice and smooth. If needed, you can add some water to thin it, or some xanthan gum to thicken it.

After it is pureed it is ready to be served.

KAPPA CARRAGEENAN GELS

Kappa carrageenan can be used to create firm, brittle gels and is especially effective at gelling dairy-based liquids. To gel, the liquid must contain either calcium or potassium that is free to bind with the kappa carrageenan.

If the base ingredient lacks calcium it can be added in the form of calcium salts like calcium lactate or calcium chloride or potassium salts like potassium citrate or potassium phosphate. For ease we will focus on dairy gels.

Kappa carrageenan can also be combined with locust bean gum to strengthen the gels and make them less elastic.

Kappa Carrageenan Gel Process

To make a gel you combine the kappa carrageenan with the liquid you would like to gel. If the liquid does not have calcium or potassium then they will need to be added.

Bring the mixture above 70°C / 158°F and as high as a boil, then pour the liquid into molds. It will begin to set around 35-60°C / 95-140°F, depending on the calcium and potassium content of the liquid. Let it cool to room temperature, or in an ice bath, and then place the gel in the refrigerator to finish setting. It should be fully set after a few hours for most mold sizes.

Once it has set, the gel can be turned out, shaped, and plated. The gel will maintain its form as long as it stays cooler than 10-20°C / 18-36°F above its setting temperature. Please be careful serving gels that are at such a high temperature since they can cause severe burns because many people expect them to be cool.

The gel will also last for a day or two in the refrigerator.

Kappa Carrageenan Gel Ratios

The amount of kappa carrageenan you use is dependent on the type of liquid you are gelling, and the firmness of the gel you are trying to create. For typical dairy gels you can use a 0.3% to 1.5% ratio. If you are adding locust bean gum, it will be in at two-thirds the weight of the kappa carrageenan.

BUTTERSCOTCH CUSTARD

I love the flavor of butterscotch and this recipe turns it into a thick, brittle gel that adds to the creaminess and heft of the butterscotch. I like to cut it into small cubes and serve it with desserts like ice cream, chocolate cake or pound cake. It can also be used with some savory dishes, as an accent to citrus glazed pork or chicken with chipotle BBQ sauce.

I usually make my own butterscotch sauce but you can use any high quality one you have on hand. To make your own, you cook 5 tablespoons of butter and 1 cup of brown sugar over medium heat until the sugar melts. Once the sugar melts, after about 5 minutes, whisk in ¾ cup heavy cream and cook for 10 minutes, whisking occasionally.

Tools Needed
Kappa carrageenan
Immersion blender
Molds or setting containers
A scale with small gram measurements

Ingredients
500 grams milk, about 2 cups
125 grams butterscotch sauce
6.2 grams kappa carrageenan, 1%

Pour the milk into a pot and add the butterscotch. Bring to a boil and puree with an immersion blender until combined well. Add the kappa carrageenan and blend well with an immersion blender. Remove from the heat and pour into molds.

Let cool at room temperature, or in an ice bath, then place in the refrigerator to finish setting.

Once fully set the gel can be turned out and cut into any shapes desired. The gel should last for several days in the refrigerator.

IOTA AND KAPPA GELS

Iota carrageenan creates elastic gels and kappa carrageenan creates brittle gels. Because of this, you can combine the two in different ratios to make many intermediate textures.

Iota and Kappa Gel Ratios

The ratio you use will depend on the elasticity and hardness you are looking for. In general, a combined 0.3% to 1.0% total weight will range from soft to hard.

A 1:1 iota to kappa ratio will create a gel of medium elasticity and a 2:1 ratio will skew towards the carrageenan with the highest concentration.

For example, if you want a soft, elastic gel, you can use 0.20% iota with 0.1% kappa. For a gel of medium hardness and medium elasticity you would start with 0.25% iota and 0.25% kappa. For a hard, mainly brittle gel, you would use 0.3% iota with 0.6% kappa.

Peanut Butter Custard Gel

This peanut butter custard gel is a great dessert on its own or it can be used as a garnish for a variety of dishes. You can tweak this recipe by substituting melted chocolate for the peanut butter.

Tools Needed
Iota carrageenan
Kappa carrageenan
Standing or immersion blender
A scale with small gram measurements

Ingredients
540 grams milk
5 grams vanilla extract
75 grams white sugar
5 grams salt
4 grams iota carrageenan, 0.5%
1.5 grams kappa carrageenan, 0.2%
180 grams smooth peanut butter

Combine the milk, vanilla, sugar and salt with a blender. Add the carrageenans and blend well to combine.

Pour the milk into a pot and bring to a boil. Whisk in the peanut butter until combined and smooth.

Pour into molds and let cool on the counter. Once they are cool, place them into the refrigerator to finish setting.

Once fully set the gel can be turned out and cut into any shapes desired. The gel should last for several days covered in the refrigerator.

GELATIN

Common Names
Gelatin, InstaGEL, Gelatina, Vegetal

Basic Ratios By Weight
0.5-1.0% soft gels
1.0-6.0% hard gels
0.4-1.0% light foams
1.0-1.7% dense foams
10% of liquid for marshmallows

Sheets per 100 Grams Liquid
0.3-0.55 sheets, soft gels
0.55-3.3 sheets, hard gels
0.2-0.55 sheets, light foams
0.55 0.9 sheets, dense foams
5.5 sheets, marshmallows

Bloom Temperature
Cold

Dispersion Temperature
Above 50°C / 122°F

Setting Temperature
Below about 30°C / 86°F, faster at colder temperatures

Melting Temperature
Depending on the concentration from 30°C / 86°F - 40°C / 104°F

Gelatin is one of the oldest "modernist" ingredients in western cooking. It is used in many childhood favorites from the ubiquitous Jell-O at family picnics to the marshmallows roasted in s'mores. Gelatin can also be used to create foams and a wide variety of gels.

Gelatin is taken from the collagen found in the bones and skin of animals. If you make a stock at home it is what gives it body and causes it to gel in the refrigerator. It is clear and colorless and when dried it is solid and brittle. When hydrated it forms a flavorless and transparent gel which easily blends into other ingredients.

HOW TO USE GELATIN

Gelatin has many different uses but there are similar steps to using it. Unlike many ingredients you first need to hydrate the gelatin before dispersing it.

Hydrating Gelatin

All gelatin has to be hydrated, or "bloomed", before it can be used. Gelatin commonly comes as a powder or in dry sheets. They are both used in a similar manner but have a few differences when hydrating.

Hydrating Powdered Gelatin
To hydrate powdered gelatin you sprinkle it in cold liquid and let it sit for 5 to 10 minutes. The gelatin and all the liquid will go into the recipe and should be taken into account.

Hydrating Gelatin Sheets
Gelatin sheets are also hydrated in a cold liquid for 5 to 10 minutes. However, once they have hydrated you squeeze the liquid

out of the sheets and it does not go into the final recipe.

Dispersing Gelatin

Once the gelatin has been hydrated you need to disperse it into the liquid you want to gel. This is typically done through whisking, either by hand or with an standing or immersion blender.

When dispersing the gelatin make sure the liquid is warm, typically above 50°C / 122°F. If you don't want to heat all of the liquid you can dissolve the gelatin in a portion of it and then combine it with the rest. You can also disperse it in water first and then mix it into the flavored liquid, though it will dilute the flavors some.

CONVERTING BETWEEN GELATIN TYPES

As mentioned previously, there are two main types of gelatin, powdered and sheet. Sheet gelatin also comes in four different strengths: bronze, silver, gold, and platinum. The strength of gelatin is measured by their "bloom strength" and each type of sheet gelatin has a different bloom strength. We've listed them, as well as Knox, the most popular brand of powdered gelatin, in the table below with their bloom strength.

However, because of the difficulty in moving between gelatin types I tend to have both powdered gelatin and sheet gelatin on hand so I can use whatever a specific recipe calls for and save myself the effort of converting.

Type	Bloom	Grams / Sheet
Bronze	125-155	3.3
Silver	160	2.5
Gold	190-220	2.0
Knox Powdered	225	-
Platinum	235-265	1.7

Because the sheets of gelatin are different sizes, they actually contain the same amount of gelling power. So if a recipe calls for "1 sheet of gelatin" you can use any type of sheet.

Powdered gelatin typically comes in ¼ ounce / 7.2 gram packets of 225 bloom strength. Four sheets of gelatin equal about one packet, so each sheet is around 1.8 grams.

If you are using a recipe that calls for 2% powdered gelatin, you can figure out the number of sheets you need to use for every 100 grams of liquid by dividing the percent by 1.8. However, this only works for small amounts because the math isn't exact and at larger volumes the small differences add up.

For a detailed look at this conversion process I highly recommend reading an article by Daniel R. Moody that goes into detail explaining how to convert from one type of gelatin to another.[20]

GELATIN GELS

Gels are the most common thing gelatin is known for. With the popularization of Jell-O, many people picture gelatin gels as firm, wiggly cubes of fruit juice. While gelatin can make this type of gel there are many more kinds of gels that can be made from it including panna cottas and other soft gels.

Gelatin Gel Ratios

When discussing gelatin ratios it can be very confusing because of the differences in the bloom strength. All of our ratios are for powdered gelatin with a bloom strength of 225 so it is easier to convert to gelatin sheets. We also give the number of sheets per 100 grams of liquid as well.

The type of gel created is dependent on how much gelatin you use. For powdered gelatin the ratios often range from 0.5% to 1.0% for soft, tender gels. For very hard, firm gels it can be used in ratios of upwards of 6% but the typical range for firmer gels is 1% to 3%.

If you are using sheet gelatin you will use 0.27-0.55 sheets per 100 grams of liquid for soft gels and 0.55 to 1.6 sheets per 100 grams of liquid for firmer gels. For very firm gels more than 3.3 sheets per 100 grams of liquid is sometimes used.

Gelatin Gel Process

Making gelatin gels is a fairly simple process. You first hydrate the gelatin in cold water for 5 to 10 minutes. If using powdered gelatin you hydrate it directly into the liquid that will be going into the recipe for 5 to 10 minutes. If using gelatin sheets you hydrate them in cold water for the same amount of time and then squeeze the water out of them once they are hydrated and it will not be added to the recipe.

Once the gelatin is hydrated you will disperse it into the liquid it will be gelling. To do this you need to heat the liquid above 50°C / 122°F and whisk or blend the gelatin into it.

After it is dispersed you pour the liquid into a mold and let it cool to set. Placing it in a refrigerator or setting the mold in an ice bath can speed up the process.

Once the gel has set in the mold you can turn it out, cut it into shapes, or serve it directly from the mold.

MARGARITA GELS

This is a more tasty take on the ubiquitous Jell-O shot especially if you top them with some candied lime peel and a little sprig of mint. You can follow this recipe but substitute any of your favorite drinks or feel free to just use a mix instead of making your own. Drinks with higher alcohol percents will sometimes need a little more gelatin to keep them the same firmness.

Be sure you bloom and disperse the gelatin in water instead of the alcohol or you could burn all the alcohol off when you heat it.

Tools Needed
Gelatin
Whisk
Mold or container for setting

Ingredients
230 grams cold water
9 gelatin sheets or 2 ¼ packets, 1.5%
350 grams tequila
230 grams fresh lime juice
120 grams Cointreau or Triple Sec

Place the water and gelatin in a pot. Let the gelatin bloom in the water for 5 to 10 minutes.

Once the gelatin is bloomed, heat the water over medium to medium-high heat while stirring until the gelatin dissolves completely. Remove the pan from the heat.

Add the tequila, lime juice, and Cointreau and whisk to combine. Pour the mixture into your mold or container and let cool. Once it has cooled slightly place it in the refrigerator for several hours.

After it is fully set you can unmold it and cut it into any shapes you like. Store them in the refrigerator until serving.

Peanut Butter Panna Cotta

Peanut butter is one of my favorite flavors and I think it goes great in this creamy panna cotta. Because of how few ingredients are in this dish, the quality of them is very important. Using good, natural peanut butter and quality maple syrup will make a huge difference in the flavor of the panna cotta.

There are countless ways to mold the panna cotta. Traditional molds, or 6 ounce molds work great. You can also plate it in wine glasses or do smaller versions in shot glasses.

Tools Needed
Gelatin
Whisk
Molds or containers for setting

Ingredients
700 grams cold whole milk
4 gelatin sheets or 1 packet, 0.75%
230 grams creamy peanut butter
120 grams maple syrup

Place the milk and gelatin in a pot. Let the gelatin bloom in the milk for 5 to 10 minutes.

Once the gelatin is bloomed, heat the milk over medium to medium-high heat while stirring until the gelatin dissolves completely. Whisk in the peanut butter and maple syrup until evenly mixed. Taste the mixture and add salt or more maple syrup as needed to balance the flavors. Remove the pan from the heat.

Pour the panna cotta into your molds and let cool on the counter. Once they have cooled, place them in the refrigerator for several hours to fully set. They will last in the refrigerator for several days and will firm up the longer they are in there.

GELATIN FOAMS

Gelatin can be used to create a variety of foams from light and airy to heavy and dense, all of which will have fine, even bubbles. All gelatin foams must be served cold or they will quickly break down as the gelatin melts.

Gelatin Foaming Process

If you have a whipping siphon, gelatin foams are very easy to make. First hydrate the gelatin and disperse it into the liquid you want to foam. Then pour the mixture into the whipping siphon and refrigerate it for several hours before dispensing.

Gelatin Foaming Ratios

The density of the foam will depend on the amount of gelatin used. Once again, all ratios are for powdered gelatin with a bloom strength of 225.

For light foams you can use powdered gelatin in a 0.4% to 1.0% ratio. For denser foams using powdered gelatin in a 1.0% to 1.7% ratio is typical. Sometimes you will see even higher ratios.

If you are using sheet gelatin you would normally use 0.2 to 0.55 sheets per 100 grams of liquid for light foams or 0.55 to 0.9 sheets per 100 grams of liquid for dense foams.

Apple Cider Foam

This foam is full of apple cider flavor and a great way to add depth and texture to different cold dishes. It's great as a topping to ice creams, on chocolate cake or even in a shot glass as an amuse bouche. My favorite dish to serve it with is a hot apple crisp topped with ice cream and the cider foam. Just remember that hot foods will melt the foam quickly.

The quality of the cider will affect the flavor of the resulting foam so if you can find good, local cider it's worth getting.

Tools Needed
Gelatin
Whisk
Whipping siphon

Ingredients
400 grams cold apple cider
2 gelatin sheets or ½ packet, 0.9%

Pour 75 to 100 grams of cider into a pot with the gelatin. Let the gelatin bloom for 5 to 10 minutes.

Once the gelatin has bloomed, heat the pot over medium to medium-high heat while stirring until the gelatin has dissolved and is evenly dispersed. Stir in the remaining cider.

Pour the cider into a whipping siphon and charge with nitrous oxide according to the manufacturer's directions. Refrigerate the whipping siphon for several hours until the gelatin sets, typically 2 to 3 hours.

Dispense the foam when you are ready to serve your dishes.

GELATIN SPONGES

Many people love gelatin sponges, in the form of marshmallows, even if they don't realize that's what they are eating.

There are many different ways to create gelatin sponges and many of them go beyond the scope of this book but we will cover how to make marshmallows.

Marshmallow Process

Making marshmallows is surprisingly easy as long as you have a standing mixer with a whisk attachment. There are two components to a marshmallow, the gelatin and water mixture, and the candy syrup.

You start by combining gelatin and either water or a flavored liquid in the bowl of the standing mixer and let the gelatin bloom for 5 to 10 minutes.

While the gelatin is blooming you make the candy syrup by combining sugar, water, and corn syrup in a pot and heating it to 110°C to 116°C / 230°F to 240°F.

Combine the syrup with the gelatin mixture and whisk on high speed for 8 to 15 minutes until the mixture triples in height. At that point you pour it out into a mold and let it cool and set at room temperature for several hours, or even overnight before cutting it into whatever shapes you prefer.

You can change the texture of the marshmallows by beating them for a longer or shorter amount of time or adding other ingredients like agar or egg whites.

You can also flavor them by adding extracts like vanilla or maple near the end of the whipping process or replacing the water in the bowl with a flavored liquid like brewed tea, or fruit juices and purees.

Marshmallow Ratios

When making marshmallows you typically want an equal weight of water and sugar. The amount of gelatin used will be around 10% of the weight of the water, or 5.5 sheets per 100 grams.

Marshmallows are a favorite food of children everywhere. These homemade ones are so much better than store bought that there is really no comparison. Whether you want to eat these on smores, in hot cocoa or just plain they will amaze you and your friends.

You can mold the marshmallows on an acetate sheet that has been sprayed with Pam using pastry bars, on a sheet pan, or in a baking pan.

Tools Needed
Standing mixer with whisk attachment
A scale with small gram measurements
Gelatin
Candy thermometer
13" x 9" baking pan or raised sheet pan

Ingredients
For the gelatin base
220 grams water
12 gelatin sheets or 3 packets, 10%

For the Mold
½ cup powdered sugar or confectioners sugar
½ cup cornstarch

For the Syrup
220 grams white sugar
100 grams water
60 grams light corn syrup

For Flavoring
1 teaspoon vanilla extract

Attach the whisk attachment to your standing mixer. Add the ingredients for the gelatin base and let the gelatin hydrate for 5 to 10 minutes.

Prepare a 13" x 9" baking pan by spraying it with Pam. Combine the cornstarch and powdered sugar and sift some of the cornstarch mixture in the pan.

While the gelatin is blooming, combine the ingredients for the syrup in a sauce pan set over medium-high to high heat. Stir it lightly until the sugar is dissolved and then leave it alone while it heats. Cook the syrup until the temperature reaches 110°C to 116°C / 230°F to 240°F.

Remove the syrup from the heat and pour it into the standing mixer on top of the bloomed gelatin and water. Turn the mixer on low and slowly increase the speed until it is on high, being careful not to splash the hot syrup out of the mixer.

Whip the marshmallow mixture until it has tripled in volume, it should take 8 to 15 minutes. When the marshmallows have almost been fully whipped, add the vanilla extract and make sure it is fully incorporated.

Pour the marshmallow mixture into the pan and spread it out evenly. Sift the top with some of the cornstarch mixture. Let the marshmallow set for several hours, preferably overnight.

Dust a cutting board with the starch powder. Turn the marshmallows out onto the cutting board and cut into the shapes you want. Coat the shapes with the cornstarch mixture to prevent them from sticking to each other.

I've found the best way to cut the marshmallows into squares is using a lightly oiled rolling pizza cutter, which I first heard suggested by Alton Brown. However, using a lightly oiled knife works well, as do kitchen shears. You can also use lightly oiled cookie cutters for unique shapes.

You can store the marshmallows for several days in a sealed container

LECITHIN

If you are interested in staying up to date with the work we are doing in modernist cooking feel free to follow us on Twitter. We post articles we find interesting, links to new recipes, and other items of interest.

We are @jasonlogsdon_sv

Lecithin is a natural emulsifier and stabilizer which comes from fatty substances found in plant and animal tissues. Many people unknowingly use it everyday because of its presence in egg yolks.

Lecithin's emulsifying properties are why egg yolks are often used to create emulsions, like mayonnaise and several sauces like Hollandaise. One end of the lecithin molecule binds to water and the other binds to oil, helping to strengthen and stabilize the emulsion.

To keep the strength of the lecithin at a constant, and to remove the flavor of the egg, lecithin is commonly used as a culinary powder. A common source of lecithin powder is soy lecithin, which is derived from soy beans either mechanically or chemically and is a byproduct of soy bean oil creation. The end product is a light brown powder that has low water solubility, meaning it dissolves easily in water.

In modernist cooking lecithin powder can be used to a similar effect to bind vinaigrettes and other stable solutions. Lecithin is also a great stabilizer and is often used in creating "airs" or other long lasting, light foams.

Lecithin is also used in pastries, confections and chocolate to enhance dough elasticity and increase moisture tolerance.

LECITHIN DISPERSION

Lecithin can be directly mixed in to the liquid at pretty much any temperature. It should be whisked in or quickly blended, an immersion blender works well.

LECITHIN FOAMS AND AIRS[21]

Creating foams and airs with lecithin is a very easy and forgiving process.

Lecithin Foam Process

To create a lecithin foam you first make a flavorful liquid. This is almost always strongly flavored because the resulting foam will lighten the flavor due to the large quantity of air incorporated.

Next, whisk or blend in the lecithin powder. You want the powder to just be dispersed and the foaming kept to a minimum. Most liquids can be kept at this stage for several hours before foaming.

The next step is to foam the liquid by introducing air and creating bubbles through agitation of some kind. Typically this is done using a whisk or immersion blender, but any type of agitator can be used including aquarium pumps, blenders, mixers with a whisk attachment and siphons.

When you are foaming the liquid remember that the goal isn't to mix or blend the liquid but to incorporate air into it. Because of this, using an immersion blender in a wide container where a quarter of the blender is out of the liquid can be ideal.

Depending on the liquid and the agitation used this will usually take 1 to 5 minutes to fully create the bubbles. You will also have liquid left in the bottom of the container.

Let the foam rest for a minute or two for the less stable bubbles to collapse. You can now use the foam as desired. It can be plated directly onto a dish, frozen to make a cold preparation, dehydrated to make a crisp, or any of a number of other uses.

The foams will usually last about 30 to 60 minutes, though they are constantly, if slowly, losing volume once they are created.

Foam Ratios

The percent of lecithin added is usually between 0.25% to 1% of the weight of the liquid, 0.6% is a good starting point if you are unsure how much to use. Using too much lecithin will actually cause the foam to collapse. The exact amount needed will depend on the specific liquid being used and how watery or oily it is, as well as how many particles are still in it.

CITRUS AIR

This is a very simple recipe that results in a versatile air. I have used citrus air in several different dishes. It's great as a topper for straight-up tequila, replacing the ubiquitous lime wedge on the rim of the glass. It can also be used to flavor fish or other foods that pair well with citrus.

It can be frozen for a very light topping that melts and dissolves instantly when placed in the mouth. The frozen air can be used on sliced strawberries or small squares of pound cake with some sweet syrup to counteract the citrus.

Tools Needed
Soy lecithin
Fresh citrus juice
Immersion blender
Flat bottomed, wide container
A scale with small gram measurements

Ingredients
200 grams fresh lime juice
100 grams fresh lemon juice
50 grams water
2.1 grams soy lecithin, 0.6%

Combine all of the ingredients well in a wide, flat bottomed container.

When ready to serve, blend the citrus mixture using an immersion blender until a nice head of foam develops. Let the citrus air sit for 1 minute to stabilize before spooning out to serve.

This recipe shows you how you can create flavored liquids that you can then easily foam. I use poblano peppers to make a spicy air that is great in Mexican inspired dishes.

You can roast the poblano peppers for additional flavor if you desire.

Tools Needed

Soy lecithin
Immersion blender
Chinois or fine strainer
Flat bottomed, wide container
A scale with small gram measurements

Ingredients

400 grams water
2 poblano peppers, roughly chopped
2.1 grams soy lecithin, 0.6%

Place the water and poblano peppers in a pot and bring to a boil. Blend with the immersion blender until combined. Remove from the heat and let steep 10 minutes.

Add the lecithin to the pot and blend with the immersion blender until it is combined. Strain the mixture through a chinois and into in a wide, flat bottomed container.

When ready to serve, blend the poblano mixture using an immersion blender until a nice head of foam develops. Let the poblano air sit for 1 minute to stabilize before spooning out to serve.

LECITHIN EMULSIONS

Creating and stabilizing emulsions is the other common use of lecithin. Egg yolks are used in many sauces and dressings because the lecithin in them holds the sauce together. Both mayonnaise and aioli are built on this idea.

However, sometimes you want the binding properties of egg yolks without adding the flavor of the egg itself. Sometime you are serving it to individuals with weak immune systems or who are vegan so you would prefer not to use raw eggs. This is when lecithin powder is a great substitute.

Lecithin powder will bind and slightly thicken the emulsion, helping it to hold longer before breaking and usually adding a subtle creamy texture to it.

Emulsifying Process

To stabilize an emulsion, weigh the liquid you want to stabilize then measure the appropriate amount of lecithin. Sprinkle the lecithin on the liquid and whisk or blend to combine. The lecithin should start binding right away, stabilizing the emulsion.

Emulsion Ratios

For an emulsion lecithin will usually be added as 0.5% to 1% of the liquid by weight. To help strengthen the emulsion you can also add some xanthan gum at a 0.1% to 0.4% ratio, which has the sometimes desired benefit of slightly thickening it.

EGGLESS CAESAR SALAD DRESSING

Caesar salad dressing is a classic, creamy dressing that holds together well because of the lecithin in the egg yolk. However, many people don't like using raw eggs in their cooking. Adding some lecithin powder helps the emulsion stay together and makes the egg yolk completely optional.

I've provided my recipe for eggless Caesar dressing but you can use any recipe that you like, then add about 0.6% lecithin by weight for stabilization.

I've also given a recommendation for xanthan gum if you would like to create a thicker dressing. With the xanthan gum I would start at the low end, blend it in and check the thickness. You don't want to over-thicken the dressing or the mouthfeel will be very poor.

The recipe makes about 1 cup of dressing.

Tools Needed
Soy lecithin
Xanthan gum, optional
Blender or food processor
A scale with small gram measurements

Ingredients
4 anchovy filets
1 tablespoon Dijon mustard
3 cloves garlic, diced
45 grams fresh lemon juice, about 3 tablespoons
45 grams grated parmesan cheese
15 grams water, about 1 tablespoon
110 grams olive oil, about ½ cup

1.1 grams soy lecithin powder, about 0.6%
Salt and pepper
0.18-0.72 grams xanthan gum, 0.1-0.4%, optional

Place all of the ingredients in a food processor or blender and process well until combined.

The dressing should hold together for a decent amount of time but it will still begin to break. I've found that giving it a good whisking right before serving can bring it back together nicely. If you thickened it with xanthan gum it will hold together even longer.

Maple Vinaigrette

Combine the vinegar, lemon juice, maple syrup, salt, and pepper in a narrow bowl or mixing container that works well with your immersion blender. Blend in the olive oil with an immersion blender or whisk attachment.

Taste the vinaigrette for seasoning and adjust the olive oil and vinegar to control the acidity.

Once the vinaigrette tastes balanced to you add the xanthan gum and lecithin then blend well to combine. Taste the vinaigrette and make sure the mouthfeel and thickness is what you prefer. Add more xanthan gum or liquid to adjust the thickness.

It is now ready to be served.

I like the sweet maple syrup with the tangy balsamic vinegar. This goes well on salads, especially ones with berries. You can also add a little more xanthan and use the vinaigrette as a sauce on fish or chicken.

Makes ½ cup

Tools Needed
Lecithin
Xanthan gum
Immersion blender
A scale with small gram measurements

Ingredients
45 grams balsamic vinegar
15 grams lemon juice
20 grams maple syrup
90 grams olive oil
Salt and pepper
1.0 grams lecithin powder, 0.6%
0.3 grams xanthan gum, 0.2%

CHICKEN CURRY SALAD

The spiciness of curry paste can really vary depending on the brand. I call for 3 teaspoons but feel free to use more or less so it matches the spice level you like. You can easily add more before blending in the xanthan gum and lecithin.

Tools Needed
Xanthan gum
Lecithin
Immersion blender
A scale with small gram measurements

Ingredients
For the Dressing
16 grams red curry paste, about 1 tablespoon
110 grams olive oil, about ½ cup
30 grams lemon juice, about 2 tablespoons
Salt and pepper
0.9 grams lecithin powder, 0.6%
0.3 grams xanthan gum, 0.2%
⅓ cup fruit chutney

For the Salad
1 celery stalk, diced
2 carrots, peeled and diced
2 tablespoons fresh chives, chopped
2 tablespoons scallions, thinly sliced
⅛ cup fresh parsley, minced
⅛ cup fresh basil, minced
2 cups seedless grapes, halved
1 apple, preferably crisp and good for eating, peeled and diced
4 chicken breasts, seared and chopped
½ cup pecans, toasted

First make the dressing. Combine the curry paste, olive oil, lemon juice, salt, and pepper in a narrow bowl or mixing container that works well with your immersion blender. Blend well with an immersion blender.

Taste the dressing for seasoning and adjust the olive oil and lemon juice to control the acidity and the red curry paste to adjust the heat level.

Once the dressing tastes balanced, add the xanthan gum and lecithin then blend well to combine. Stir in the fruit chutney.

Mix all of the salad ingredients except for the pecans in a bowl and toss well with the dressing.

Sprinkle the pecans on top and serve.

MALTODEXTRIN

Maltodextrin has gained culinary fame by its ability to turn oils and fats into powders. It is also often used as a thickener and stabilizer of high-fat ingredients, as well as a way to help disperse other ingredients like transglutaminase that can clump on their own.

Maltodextrin is a sweet polysaccharide that is produced from starch, corn, wheat, tapioca or potato through partial hydrolysis and spray drying. A very common type for cooking is tapioca maltodextrin. It is a very, very light powder that can absorb water as well as oil.

It is often used as an additive because it has fewer calories than sugar and is easily absorbed and digested by the body in the form of glucose. It also helps lock in aromas, making dishes more fragrant.

It can also be used to dust over sticky surfaces such as marshmallows to keep them from sticking together without altering their flavors.

There are many varieties that maltodextrin comes in but I prefer to use the N-Zorbit M brand.

MALTODEXTRIN FAT POWDERS

There are a few things to keep in mind when making fat powders and pastes from maltodextrin but in general it is a simple and forgiving process.

Maltodextrin Ratios

Maltodextrin is a pretty forgiving ingredient when you make powders and pastes and you can easily add more until you have the texture you desire. The amount used will also depend on the fat you are trying to thicken.

In general, you will use a 30% to 45% weight ratio for pastes and 45% to 60% for powders. It is best to start with a smaller amount of maltodextrin and add more until you have reached the texture you desire. It is helpful to reserve some of the fat in case you add too much maltodextrin.

Maltodextrin Powdering Process

Creating powders and pastes from fats is easy using maltodextrin. You combine the liquid fat with the maltodextrin and mix well, adding more fat or maltodextrin until it is the texture you desire. Using a whisk or fork for the mixing will usually be good enough.

For finer powders you can push the resulting paste through a tamis or fine-meshed sieve. The resulting powders and pastes can also be formed into shapes and baked.

Most powders will last about a day at room temperature or several days in the refrigerator.

Sources of Fat

There are many places to get fat from. Some of the most common are off the shelf oils such as olive oil, peanut oil, or other flavored oils. You can also render the fat from bacon, chicken, pork, duck, or other foods and turn that into a powder that will carry many of the same flavors.

Creating Flavored Oils

To create unlimited powders and pastes remember that you can infuse oils with many different flavors before turning them into a powder. You can cook garlic and red pepper flakes over low heat in olive oil for a spicy, roasted garlic olive oil. You can infuses oil with vanilla for a sweet powder.

A common technique for infusing oils with more mild ingredients, such as carrots or bell peppers, is to heat the ingredient in oil until it is soft and the oil is perfumed with the scent. Transfer the oil to a blender and blend until smooth. Run the oil through a chinois or cheesecloth to strain it. You can then turn the flavored oil into a paste or powder, or even just use it as is.

The options are truly unlimited.

This sesame powder comes together really quickly and is a great visual addition to many dishes. It also adds an interesting textural element to more traditional plates. It can be used with any dish that a drizzle of sesame oil would go well with, including many Asian foods.

Tools Needed
Tapioca maltodextrin
Whisk or fork
Bowl
Sesame oil
A scale with small gram measurements

Ingredients
100 grams sesame oil

3 grams salt

20 - 50 grams tapioca maltodextrin, the actual amount will depend on the quality and type of sesame oil you use, 20%-50%

Pour the sesame oil into a bowl large enough to comfortably hold it. Whisk in the salt.

To turn the sesame oil into powder begin to whisk in the tapioca maltodextrin. Once it begins to thicken and clump you can add it in more slowly and you may have to start using a fork to incorporate the maltodextrin as whisks will often fill with the paste. Continue to add tapioca maltodextrin while mixing until it forms the texture you want.

When you are ready to serve the sesame powder simply spoon or sprinkle it over the dish.

The powder will last for several hours at room temperature or in the refrigerator for several days.

This roasted garlic olive oil paste has many uses. I love to serve it as a spread for freshly baked Italian bread since it delivers a texture and flavor that isn't expected. It can also be used as a topping for fish or even meats.

I call for the garlic cloves to be thinly sliced, this allows you to use them as a flavorful, crunchy garnish but if you do not want them as a garnish you can save time by coarsely chopping them.

You can change up the flavors as you see fit. Adding some sage or rosemary to the oil would add even more flavor to it or you could go in a Mexican direction by toasting dried chile peppers in the oil instead of the garlic.

Tools Needed

Tapioca maltodextrin
Whisk or fork
Sesame oil
A scale with small gram measurements
Chinois or cheesecloth

Ingredients

100 grams olive oil
3 grams salt
10 cloves garlic, peeled and thinly sliced
1 teaspoon red pepper flakes
20 - 50 grams tapioca maltodextrin, the actual amount will depend on the quality and type of olive oil you use, 20%-50%

Combine the olive oil, salt, garlic, and red pepper flakes in a pan over low to medium-low heat. Let cook until the garlic has browned nicely and the oil smells and tastes like garlic and pepper.

Remove the garlic and reserve for a garnish. Strain the infused olive oil through a chinois or cheesecloth into a bowl large enough to comfortably hold it.

To turn the olive oil into a paste begin to whisk in the tapioca maltodextrin. Once it begins to thicken and clump you can add it in more slowly and you may have to start using a fork to incorporate the maltodextrin as whisks will often fill with the paste. Continue to add tapioca maltodextrin while mixing until it forms the texture you desire.

When you are ready to serve the roasted garlic olive oil paste simply spread it using a knife.

The paste will remain in good condition for several hours at room temperature or in the refrigerator for several days.

METHYLCELLULOSE

Methylcellulose is one of the most interesting modernist ingredients. It has the unusual property of gelling when it is heated and melting as it cools. One of the most dramatic uses of this is "instant noodles" when the diner has a squeeze bottle full of liquid that when squeezed into a soup instantly turns into noodles. It has also been used to make "hot ice cream" that melts as it cools.

In addition, it is often employed as a binder in coatings, such as fried chicken batter, because it will solidify as soon as it hits the oil, creating a barrier that keeps the oil out and the juices in. Methylcellulose can also be used to stabilize foams and emulsions.

Methylcellulose is made from cellulose pulp, which is taken from plants' cell walls. There are about 20 kinds of methylcellulose and while similar, they all have different properties. Because of this, we will only cover two here.

Methocel F50 is commonly used to stabilize foams. Methocel A4C gels at a lower temperature and is good in batters and coatings. Both of these were recommended by Ideas in Food and I've found them to be more than enough to keep me busy exploring this style of cooking.

DISPERSION AND HYDRATION

Methylcellulose is typically dispersed in hot liquids, above the setting temperature of the type you are using. Some, like Methocel F50, can also be dispersed in cold water if using a blender.

Once the methylcellulose has been dispersed, you need to cool the liquid in order for it to hydrate. The hydration temperature varies for the different types but a good rule of thumb is below 15°C / 59°F. Most types need to stay at this temperature for about an hour. I typically let the liquid cool on the counter or in an ice bath and then refrigerate it for several hours to be on the safe side.

Smelly Liquid
Some forms of methylcellulose react poorly to sugar and result in a bad smell, similar to

a wet dog or corked wine. Ideas in Food, with credit to Harold McGee, have come up with a solution. If this occurs you can line the container you are hydrating the methylcellulose in with plastic wrap, which will absorb the odor from the mixture so the resulting foam or gel will not smell.

METHYLCELLULOSE FOAMS

Methocel F50 is known as being a great stabilizer of foams so I will focus on it in this section. It can be used both for fresh, raw foams as well as foams that are cooked or dehydrated. Xanthan gum is also often added to help the foam hold its shape.

Methocel F50 Foaming Process

Regardless of what type of foam you are going to make, the beginning of the process is the same. Methocel F50 can be hydrated in cold liquids in a standing blender. Add the liquid you want to foam to the blender and blend it at a speed where a vortex forms. Sprinkle the Methocel F50 into the vortex, along with any other ingredients like xanthan gum. Continue blending for another minute or two.

Place the mixture in the refrigerator for several hours. The Methocel F50 will not begin to hydrate until it gets below about 15°C / 59°F . The hydration is also a slow process which is why the extended cooling time is suggested.

Once the Methocel F50 has hydrated add the mixture to a stand mixer with a whisk attachment. Whisk the mixture until peaks are formed. You can whip to either soft or stiff peaks, depending on the presentation and texture you want. The foam is now ready to be used.

For a more refined presentation you can scoop the foam into a pastry bag, or a ziploc bag with a corner cut off, and pipe it into bite-sized mounds or long trails of foam.

To make meringues, you can place the foam in a dehydrator and dehydrate it for 3 to 5 hours, until it is nice and crisp. An oven set to low with the door slightly ajar also works well for dehydrating them.

Methocel F50 Foaming Ratios

In general, a ratio of 1.0% to 2.0% Methocel F50 is combined with a ratio of 0.1% to 0.3% xanthan gum. The higher the amount of Methocel F50 and xanthan gum the denser the foam will be.

Both the *Ideas in Food* and *Modernist Cuisine* books suggest using 1.0% Methocel F50 and 0.15% xanthan gum for a standard foam and that is my go-to ratio as well.

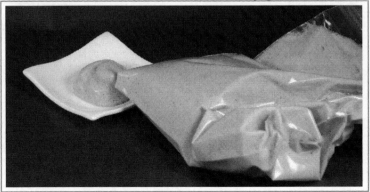

This is a standard foam recipe using Methocel F50 and xanthan gum. You can vary the liquid to be whatever you need for your dish. The cherry foam is awesome with a seared duck breast and pecans, or even on chocolate cake or cherry pie.

Tools Needed
Methocel F50
Xanthan gum
Standing blender
Standing mixer with whisk attachment
Pastry bag or ziploc bag, optional
A scale with small gram measurements

Ingredients
200 grams cherry juice
Sugar or honey, optional
2 grams Methocel F50, 1.0%
0.3 grams xanthan gum, 0.15%

Taste the cherry juice and if it needs sweetening add some sugar or honey to balance the flavors.

Place the cherry juice in a standing blender and turn it on to a speed where a vortex forms. Sprinkle the Methocel F50 and xanthan gum into the vortex and continue to blend for 30 to 60 seconds to ensure even dispersion. Place the cherry juice in the refrigerator for several hours to hydrate.

Once fully hydrated, remove the cherry juice mixture from the refrigerator and whip it with the standing mixer until peaks form, about 5 to 10 minutes. Once the peaks have formed the foam is ready to be served.

You can serve the foam by spooning it directly onto the dish. For a more refined presentation you can spoon it into a pastry bag or a ziploc bag with the corner cut off and pipe out small mounds or a long line of foam.

These meringues are easy to make and are a great snack. They are also a wonderful garnish for fish or salads. You can make them with almost any type of fruit juice or other flavored liquid.

Tools Needed

Methocel F50
Xanthan gum
Standing blender
Standing mixer with whisk attachment
Dehydrator or oven
Pastry bag or ziploc bag
A scale with small gram measurements

Ingredients

100 grams orange juice, pulp free
100 grams pineapple juice, pulp free
Sugar or honey, optional
2 grams Methocel F50, 1.0%
0.3 grams xanthan gum, 0.15%

Combine the juices in a standing blender. Taste the juices and if they need sweetening add some sugar or honey to balance the flavors.

Turn the blender on to a speed where a vortex forms. Sprinkle the Methocel F50 and xanthan gum into the vortex and continue to blend for 30 to 60 seconds to ensure even dispersion. Place the juice in the refrigerator for several hours to hydrate.

Once fully hydrated, remove the juice from the refrigerator and whip it with the standing mixer until peaks form, about 5 to 10 minutes.

Spoon the foam into a pastry bag or a ziploc bag with the corner cut off.

Using a Dehydrator

Line a dehydrator tray with a silicone mat or parchment paper. Pipe small mounds onto the tray. Dehydrate for 3 to 5 hours, until it turns crispy and is fully dehydrated.

Using an Oven

Line a sheet pan or cookie sheet with a silicone mat or parchment paper. Pipe small mounds onto the tray. Set the oven to low, place the meringues into it, and leave the door slightly ajar. Let the meringues dehydrate for 2 to 6 hours, until they turn crispy and are fully dehydrated.

Methylcellulose Gels

Most types of methylcellulose can create gels. The gels are thermo-reversible, meaning they can be set and unset multiple times. As discussed above, in contrast to most gels, the methylcellulose gel will set as it heats and then unset when it cools off.

For this section we will focus on creating gels with Methocel A4C because it has a lower setting and melting temperature then many other types, making it easier to work with for some preparations.

Methocel A4C Gelling Process

Methocel A4C has to be dispersed in a hot liquid so the first step is to bring the liquid you want to gel to a boil. Then whisk or blend in the Methocel A4C. You can also disperse the Methocel A4C in water first and blend that into another liquid if you don't want to heat it.

When the Methocel A4C is dispersed evenly you need to cool the liquid and then refrigerate it for the hydration to begin. It won't start to hydrate until the temperature is below about 15°C / 59°F and it usually takes at least 30 to 60 minutes to hydrate.

Once the liquid has hydrated it can be gelled by raising the temperature above 50°C to 55°C / 122°F to 131°F. This can be done in a variety of ways, from deep frying to baking, or piping it directly into hot liquids.

Methocel A4C Gelling Ratios

When creating gels with Methocel A4C you typically will use a 0.25% to 3.0% ratio, depending on how firm of a gel you desire.

Instant Mushroom Noodles

These instant noodles make for an awesome presentation. They are created in the bowl of soup in front of the diner, or the diner can even make the noodles themselves. They are based off of Wylie Dufresne's instant tofu noodles.

They go very well with any clear broth soups. I especially like them as the noodles in chicken noodle soup but they also work great with miso or steak soups as well. You could even use them in a minestrone.

Tools Needed
Methocel A4C
Oven
Standing blender
Immersion blender
A scale with small gram measurements

Ingredients
225 grams baby bella mushrooms, cleaned
Olive oil
Salt and pepper
100 grams water
6.5 grams Methocel A4C, 2%
4-6 sage leaves

Hot chicken soup, for serving

Preheat the oven to 204°C / 400°F.

Place the mushrooms on a sheet pan with raised edges. Drizzle with olive oil and sprinkle with salt and pepper. Roast for 15 to 30 minutes, until they begin to brown and have released most of their juices. Remove from the oven.

Heat the water to a boil. Sprinkle in the Methocel A4C and mix with the immersion blender. Remove from the heat and let cool slightly.

Combine the water, mushrooms, and sage leaves in the standing blender. Puree until it becomes a smooth mixture then cool and place in the refrigerator for several hours for the Methocel A4C to hydrate.

Once hydrated fully, pour the mixture into a squeeze bottle. Let it come to room temperature before serving. For serving, make sure you have a very hot soup because the noodles will not gel unless they are raised above 50°C to 55°C / 122°F to 131°F.

To serve, place the nozzle of the squeeze bottle just below the surface of the soup and squeeze some of the mixture out while moving the bottle around. It will gel almost instantly, forming the mushroom noodles.

Sodium Alginate

If you are interested in staying up to date with modernist cooking you can join our free newsletter and get monthly modernist cooking tips and links to the best articles on the internet.

You can join our newsletter here:
http://is.gd/Jwiwij

In many ways sodium alginate has become the poster child for modernist cooking due to its use in spherification. Despite being used as an example of the "chemicals" used in molecular gastronomy it is actually a natural gelling agent taken from the cell walls of brown algae.

It easily disperses, hydrates, and gels in any temperature of liquid. Sodium alginate gels when it comes in contact with calcium. It also has many uses other than spherification such as thickening and general gelling.

Sodium alginate works best in non-acidic mixtures. If you are trying to use it in something acidic you can usually add sodium citrate to alter the pH before adding the sodium alginate.

REVERSE SPHERIFICATION

I personally find reverse spherification to be much easier to do than direct spherification[22]. Because you can freeze the flavored liquid base it is much easier to make perfect looking spheres than when trying to pour it directly into the setting bath. Since the gelling process occurs on the outside of the liquid you also run no risk of gelling all the liquid so you do not have to serve it right away.

Reverse Spherification Process

In reverse spherification you add calcium to the flavored liquid you want to gel, called the "base". The calcium is usually added in the form of calcium lactate or calcium chloride. Calcium lactate is almost always used in reverse spherification because it has a much more neutral taste than the bitter calcium chloride. Once the calcium has been added you freeze the base in spherical or hemispherical molds.

Next, the sodium alginate is mixed with water, and sometimes sugar, to form a setting bath. The frozen spheres of base are then placed into the bath for 1 to 5 minutes, depending on the thickness of the membrane you want. Make sure the spheres are not touching or they will fuse together.

I recommend starting with one sphere at a time to test out some different setting lengths. That way you can see which one works best for your specific purpose. In general I've found:

- Small Spheres - 2 minutes
- Medium Spheres - 4 minutes
- Large Spheres - 5 minutes
- Thin membrane - 1 minute
- Medium Membrane - 3 minutes
- Thick Membrane - 5 minutes

Once the membranes have set the spheres are removed and rinsed in a water bath. This bath can be warm or cold, depending on the temperature you would like to serve the spheres.

The spheres can be stored for several hours or even overnight. However, the water bath can leech out some of the flavor so they shouldn't be left in the water bath for more than 15 to 30 minutes. If you know you will be storing them for an extended period of time I recommend setting aside some of the liquid used in the base, before the calcium is added, and storing the spheres in it.

These spheres can be served either cold or hot, up to about 130°C / 266°F. Please be careful serving spheres that are at such a high temperature because they can cause severe burns since many people expect them to be cooler.

You can also place the finished spheres into a whipping siphon, with some reserved calcium-free liquid, charge it, and let me sit for several hours to create carbonated spheres.

Reverse Spherification Ratios

For the flavored base a ratio of 1.0% to 3.0% calcium lactate is typically used with a setting bath of 0.4-0.5% sodium alginate.

This basic recipe for mango spheres can be applied to almost any non-acidic fruit or vegetable juice. The spheres can be served cold on a salad or with vegetables. They are also good when heated and served as a flavorful topping to fish or chicken, especially if you add some hot sauce and cumin to the mango juice. This recipe will make 25 to 40 spheres.

Tools Needed
Sodium alginate
Calcium lactate
Immersion blender
Slotted spoon
Hemispherical or spherical molds
A scale with small gram measurements

Ingredients
For the Mango Spheres
400 grams mango juice, preferably fresh
8 grams calcium lactate, 2.0%

For the Alginate Bath
1000 grams water
65 grams sugar
5 grams sodium alginate, 0.5%

Combine the mango juice and calcium lactate in a bowl using an immersion blender. If the mango juice has a lot of pulp strain it out. Pour the mango juice into hemispherical or spherical molds and freeze them.

Prepare the alginate bath by placing the water, sugar, and sodium alginate in a pot. Blend well with an immersion blender and bring it to a boil. Set it aside and let it cool.

Fill another bowl with water and set aside for use as the rinsing bowl.

Place the frozen mango spheres into the alginate bath, making sure they do not touch each other. Let them set for 2 to 4 minutes. Remove them with a slotted spoon and place them into the rinsing bath. Swirl them gently to rinse off the outsides.

They will last for about 30 minutes in the water bath, or over night in reserved mango juice. They can be served hot or cold.

CARROT SPHERES

These carrot spheres can be a very interesting side to serve with different meals. For an even more unusual presentation you can place sauteed pancetta cubes in the molds when you fill them with the carrot juice. This recipe will make 25 to 40 spheres.

Tools Needed

Sodium alginate
Calcium lactate
Immersion blender
Slotted spoon
Hemispherical or spherical molds
A scale with small gram measurements

Ingredients

For the Carrot Spheres
400 grams carrot juice, preferably fresh
8 grams calcium lactate, 2.0%

For the Alginate Bath
1000 grams water
65 grams sugar
5 grams sodium alginate, 0.5%

Combine the carrot juice and calcium lactate in a bowl using an immersion blender. If the carrot juice has a lot of pulp strain it out. Pour the carrot juice into hemispherical or spherical molds and freeze them.

Prepare the alginate bath by placing the water, sugar, and sodium alginate in a pot. Blend well with an immersion blender and bring it to a boil. Set it aside and let it cool.

Fill another bowl with water and set aside for use as the rinsing bowl.

Place the frozen carrot spheres into the alginate bath, making sure they do not touch each other. Let them set for 2 to 4 minutes. Remove them with a slotted spoon and place them into the rinsing bath. Swirl them gently to rinse off the outsides.

They will last for about 30 minutes in the water bath, or over night in reserved carrot juice. They can be served hot or cold.

DIRECT SPHERIFICATION

I prefer reverse spherification for most applications but it does have its drawbacks, especially when it comes to creating small "caviar" beads. The beads will often stick to each other and clump so turning to direct spherification is usually much easier.

Direct Spherification Process

In direct spherification you combine sodium alginate with the liquid base you want to spherify and the calcium is added to the setting bath.

The sodium alginate base is then poured, spoonful by spoonful, or drop by drop, into the setting bath. After 1 to 3 minutes the spheres are removed and rinsed off. They must be served within 5 to 10 minutes because they will continue to gel as time goes on.

Direct Spherification Ratios

For direct spherification a 0.5% to 1% sodium alginate base is used with a 0.5% to 1% calcium lactate setting bath.

Using miniature spheres, referred to as caviar, is a great way to add little bursts of flavor to dishes. Here we use a chipotle water but you can use the same technique on any liquid that doesn't contain calcium.

These caviar are great additions to a tortilla soup or when placed on top of a Mexican spiced flank steak or grilled chicken. You could even use them as a garnish for Bloody Marys. Use as many chipotles as you want, or even just some hot sauce, but remember the diner will get a burst of the spice so it shouldn't be too strong.

You have to move quickly during the final steps of making these caviar because they set very quickly and continue gelling. Sometimes it can help if two people work together, one dripping in the chipotle water and the other fishing them out.

Tools Needed
Sodium alginate
Calcium lactate
Immersion blender
Slotted spoon
Plastic syringe, squeeze bottle, or eye dropper
A scale with small gram measurements

Ingredients
For the Chipotle Caviar
400 grams water
1 to 4 chipotle chiles in adobo sauce, to taste
4 grams sodium alginate, 1.0%

For the Setting Bath
1000 grams water
5 grams calcium lactate, 0.5%

Add the water and chipotle chiles to a pot and blend well with an immersion blender. Bring to a boil. Taste for spiciness, adding more chipotle peppers and pureeing if needed. Remove from the heat. Add the sodium alginate and blend with an immersion blender. Let cool and then refrigerate for several hours or overnight so the bubbles disperse.

Make the setting bath by adding the calcium lactate to the water and blending with a clean immersion blender. Fill another bowl with water to use as the rinsing bath.

Just before serving, prepare the caviar. Slowly drip the chipotle water into the setting bath using the syringe, squeeze bottle or eye dropper. After 30-45 seconds take out the caviar with the slotted spoon, place them in the rinsing bath, and swirl them around gently. Repeat until you have used all the chipotle water.

Serve the caviar as quickly as possible because they will continue to solidify.

Xanthan Gum

You can also get a lot of this modernist cooking information
on your mobile phone if you have an iPhone, iPad or an Android.

You can get more information at:
www.modernistcookingmadeeasy.com/molecular-gastronomy-app

or search the app store for "molecular gastronomy"

XANTHAN GUM AT A GLANCE

Common Names
Xanthan, Xanthan Gum, Xantana, Keltrol

Basic Ratios By Weight
0.1-0.3% thin sauce
0.3-1.0% thick sauce
0.2-0.8% foams
0.1-0.5% emulsion stabilization

Dispersion Temperature
Any

Hydration Temperature
Any

Xanthan gum, or just xanthan, is one of the easiest ingredients to work. It is used extensively to thicken liquids and is a great ingredient to use to turn thin liquids into savory sauces.

It can hydrate or disperse at any temperature, and does so quickly, making it one of the few ingredients you can add slowly and instantly see the result.

Xanthan gum is produced through the fermentation of glucose with a bacteria found in cabbage, known as Xanthomonas campesteris.

When used as a thickener in low dosages, xanthan gum produces a weak gel with high viscosity. This gel will also be thixotropic or shear thinning with a high pourability. This means that when the gel is at rest it maintains its shape but when stirred or mixed it begins to flow again as a liquid and then resets once the agitation stops.

Xanthan gum has a very neutral flavor so it mixes well with foods without masking their flavor. It provides an improved mouth feel to preparations, slightly thickening a liquid similar to how traditionally reducing a liquid does.

USES OF XANTHAN GUM

Often times the presence of bubbles within thickened liquids creates light and creamy textures. Xanthan gum also displays excellent stabilizing abilities that allow for particle suspension, which can create many interesting presentations.

Xanthan gum is gluten free and is often used as a substitute in baking and thickening. It also helps baked goods to retain more moisture than they would have otherwise.

In addition it prevents syneresis, the leaking out of water, in gels and emulsions. When mixed into products that will be frozen it helps prevent ice formation and crystallization, which leads to a more stable product during the freeze-thaw process.

When mixed into batters or tempura xanthan gum adds good cling, allowing the batter to stick more easily to the food.

Xanthan gum does not lose its properties when microwaved.

DISPERSION AND HYDRATION

Xanthan gum is very easy to disperse and hydrate.

Dispersing the Xanthan Gum
Dispersing xanthan gum is very easy and can be done in liquids of any temperature. It can typically be mixed in using a whisk,

though an immersion or standing blender works best.

You can also improve the dispersion of xanthan gum by first mixing it with sugar, then adding it to the liquid. This is similar to making a slurry out of flour and cold water before adding it to gravy to prevent clumping. The sugar will prevent the xanthan gum from hydrating until it has been dispersed enough in the liquid for the sugar percent to go down.

Hydrating the Xanthan Gum

Xanthan gum will pretty much hydrate in liquid of any temperature. However, if the liquid is very sugary then it can have trouble hydrating. Typically, if the sugar is less than 55% to 60% it will work fine.

THICKENING WITH XANTHAN GUM

One of the primary uses of xanthan gum is to thicken liquids. This can range from very minor thickening to creating very thick syrups depending on the other ingredients and the amount of xanthan gum used.

Another benefit of thickening with xanthan gum is that it greatly increases particle suspension. This means if you have herbs, spices, or other items in the liquid then the addition of xanthan gum will help keep them in suspension instead of settling to the bottom or rising to the top.

Xanthan Gum Thickening Process

To thicken a liquid with xanthan gum you just combine the xanthan gum with the liquid you want to thicken by whisking or blending. The liquid will thicken very quickly.

For thicker sauces that have been sitting you can stir or whisk them briefly to make them flow better, this is called shear-thinning. Once they have been plated they will regain their previous viscosity as long as they haven't been heated to too high of a temperature.

Most thickened liquids will keep for a day or two in the refrigerator.

Xanthan Gum Thickening Ratios

The amount of xanthan gum you will use depends on how much you would like to thicken the liquid. In general, you will use a 0.2% weight ratio for light thickening, 0.7% for a thicker sauce, and up to 1.5% for a very thick sauce.

Be warned though, adding too much xanthan gum can result in a texture and mouthfeel resembling mucus.

This balsamic vinegar syrup helps to showcase the thickening benefits of xanthan gum. It is simply a mixture of good balsamic vinegar with some honey to sweeten it. Adding the xanthan gum thickens it into a syrup without altering the flavor like reducing it in a traditional manner would. Feel free to tweak the amount of honey based on the sweetness of the balsamic vinegar you are using.

Tools Needed
Xanthan gum
Immersion or standing blender
A scale with small gram measurements

Ingredients
150 grams good balsamic vinegar, about ⅔ cup
20 grams honey, about 1 tablespoon
1.7 grams xanthan gum, 1.0%

Combine all of the ingredients in a container that can hold them comfortably. Blend them together using an immersion blender until they form the xanthan gum balsamic vinegar syrup. You can easily adjust the thickness of the syrup by adding more balsamic vinegar or xanthan gum as needed.

The xanthan gum balsamic vinegar syrup will last for several hours in a useable state. It can also be refrigerated for a few days.

When ready to serve spoon or drizzle the syrup onto your dish. It is great over strawberries with some mint, or as a sauce for ribs.

This orange sauce is one of my favorites. It combines the sweet acidity of orange juice with a little heat from the chipotles. If you prefer a more mild sauce feel free to omit the chipotles.

I love searing some steak or chicken, cutting them into chunks, and mixing it into this sauce to be served over rice. It's also great as a dressing for a spicy chopped salad.

This recipe uses xanthan gum to help thicken the sauce without having to reduce it. It also helps coat the food you end up using it on much better.

Tools Needed
Xanthan gum
Immersion blender
A scale with small gram measurements

Ingredients
40 grams sesame oil, about 3 tablespoons
3 scallions, thinly sliced
1 tablespoon garlic, minced
1 tablespoon fresh ginger, minced
1-2 chipotle chiles in adobo sauce, or a few drops
   of chipotle hot sauce
355 grams orange juice, about 1½ cups
30 grams soy sauce, about 2 tablespoons
40 grams honey, about 2 tablespoons
Salt and pepper
475 grams mandarin oranges, about 2 cups
3.7 grams xanthan gum, 0.4%

Heat a pot over medium heat.

Add the oil and scallions to the pot and cook for 1 to 2 minutes. Add the garlic and ginger and cook for 1 to 2 minutes more.

Add the chipotle chiles, orange juice, soy sauce, honey, salt, pepper, and a quarter of the Mandarin oranges and blend with the immersion blender.

Sprinkle in the xanthan gum and blend well. Stir in the remaining mandarin oranges.

It is now ready to be served.

CUBAN MOJO SAUCE

Mojo sauce is a traditional cuban sauce often used for marinating pork but it works well as a sauce too. It often uses sour orange juice but we substitute ½ normal orange juice and ½ lime juice because sour orange juice can be hard to find.

This sauce was made for pork but it is also fantastic on a grilled steak. We also use the mojo as a mop when we grill pork chops to add flavor to them.

We find that adding a touch of xanthan gum helps the sauce to cling to the meat better both during cooking and when serving.

Tools Needed
Xanthan gum
Standing or immersion blender
A scale with small gram measurements

Ingredients
40 grams olive oil, about 3 tablespoons
8 cloves garlic, minced
78 grams orange juice, about ⅓ cup
78 grams lime juice, about ⅓ cup
1 teaspoon ground cumin
Salt and pepper
1 tablespoon chopped fresh oregano
0.2 grams xanthan gum, 0.1%

To prepare the mojo sauce heat the olive oil and garlic in a pan over medium-high heat. Cook until the garlic begins to soften, about 1 minute, then add the orange juice, lime juice and cumin. Bring to a simmer and mix well. Salt and pepper to taste.

Remove from the heat and let cool slightly. Pour into a blender or a container that works well with your immersion blender.

Sprinkle in the xanthan gum and blend well. Stir in the oregano. The sauce is now ready to be used.

ROASTED TOMATO SALSA

There is something about roasted tomatoes that I really love. I combine them with some thyme and garlic for base flavor and vinegar, brown sugar, and chipotles for high notes.

I like to serve this over grilled chicken or steak but it is also a good topping for roasted asparagus or steamed green beans.

Roasted tomato salsa can be pretty watery, depending on the type of tomatoes used. I like to add a little bit of xanthan gum to thicken it up when that happens. I give the measurements for 0.2% and 0.6% but use your judgment to tailor the salsa to your own preferences.

Tools Needed
Xanthan gum
Standing or immersion blender
A scale with small gram measurements

Ingredients
½ yellow onion, diced
800 grams tomatoes, roughly diced, about 5 large
    tomatoes
1 tablespoon fresh thyme
5 garlic cloves, diced
30 grams cider vinegar, about 2 tablespoons
26 grams brown sugar, about 2 tablespoons
¼-1 teaspoon chipotle chile powder, or chile
    powder of your choice
1.6-4.8 grams xanthan gum, 0.2-0.6%

Preheat the oven to 204°C / 400°F.

Add the onion and tomatoes to a sheet pan with raised sides then sprinkle with the thyme and garlic. Bake in the oven until they soften and begin to brown, 15 to 20 minutes.

Remove from the heat and pour ¾ of it into a blender or a container that works well with your immersion blender. Stir in the cider vinegar, brown sugar, and chipotle powder. Let cool slightly.

Blend the tomato mixture to a smooth puree. Sprinkle in some of the xanthan gum and blend well to combine. Taste it for thickness and mouthfeel. If you need it thicker, continue adding xanthan gum and blending well until it has the thickness and mouthfeel you prefer.

Stir in the remaining tomato and onion mixture.

ASIAN CITRUS SAUCE

This is a very easy sauce to put together and it has a lot of nuanced flavor. Instead of the chile powder you can use a chipotle in adobo sauce or a drop or two of hot sauce.

I love this sauce on short ribs or a steak that has been coated with Chinese 5-spice powder before being grilled. I often use some orange zest and scallions as a garnish.

Tools Needed

Xanthan gum
Standing or immersion blender
A scale with small gram measurements

Ingredients

30 grams rice wine vinegar, about 2 tablespoons
60 grams orange juice, about 4 tablespoons
28 grams peanut oil or olive oil, about 2
    tablespoons
60 grams oyster sauce, about 4 tablespoons
26 grams brown sugar, about 2 tablespoons
1 teaspoon chipotle chile powder, or chile
    powder of your choice
Salt and pepper
0.8 grams xanthan gum, 0.4%

Place all of the ingredients except the xanthan gum into a blender or a container that works well with your immersion blender. Blend and taste for seasonings and make sure the balance of the flavors is good, adding more sugar, vinegar, or salt as needed.

Sprinkle in the xanthan gum and blend well to combine. Taste it for thickness and mouthfeel. If you need it thicker, continue adding xanthan gum and blending well until it has the thickness and mouthfeel you prefer.

PEACH PUREE

One of my favorite things to eat, especially during spring and summer, is fresh fruit. Whether it's whole or made into a sauce or puree, it's hard to beat the fresh flavors you get.

My only complaint with making many types of fruit purees is that they get too watery. Luckily, using a touch of xanthan gum solves this problem by slightly thickening it up and giving it a great mouthfeel. The puree is great to eat as is, or over top of french toast, a pound cake, or angel food cake.

The Amaretto adds a little background flavor but it is completely optional. You could also add some honey, champaign, or anything else tasty you have on hand.

Feel free to puree more or less of the peaches, depending on how chunky you like your puree. Be sure to adjust the xanthan gum respectively since it only needs to go into the pureed peaches. You don't even have to weigh the xanthan gum, just be careful putting it in, it's strong!

Tools Needed
Xanthan gum
Immersion or standing blender
A scale with small gram measurements

Ingredients
2 large peaches, de-pitted and coarsely chopped, about 400 grams
15 grams Amaretto or triple sec, about 1 tablespoon
A sprinkle of xanthan gum, about 0.4 grams, 0.1%, up to 1.2 grams, 0.3%
1 large peach, diced, about 200 grams

Place the coarsely chopped peaches and the Amaretto into the blending container and puree until smooth.

Starting with a small amount, sprinkle in some of the xanthan gum and blend until distributed. Test for thickness. If you want it to be thicker, sprinkle in a little more xanthan gum and blend again. Repeat until the desired thickness is reached, usually it should cling to a spoon but still flow very easily.

If the puree becomes too thick you can puree another peach in it or add some water or another liquid.

Once the puree is the thickness you want, stir in the diced peach and serve.

Xanthan Gum Foams

Since xanthan gum thickens liquids they can more easily trap air bubbles and stabilize foams.

Xanthan Gum Foaming Process

The first step to make a xanthan gum foam from a liquid is to mix in the xanthan gum using an immersion or standing blender. Once it's evenly dispersed you need to introduce air into the liquid. This can be done through whipping, blending, or with a whipping siphon. Typically a whipping siphon is the most efficient way to create a foam.

Another interesting way to create a xanthan gum foam is through the use of an aquarium bubbler. It will create large, unevenly sized bubbles, resembling soap bubbles, that can add a whimsical quality to many dishes. For this preparation it is typically combined with

Xanthan Gum Foaming Ratios

A ratio between 0.2% and 0.8% is typically used. The more xanthan gum you use the larger the bubbles that can occur, and the denser the foam will be.

For bubbles, resembling soap bubbles, a typical ratio is 0.1% to 0.4% xanthan gum and 0.2% to 2.0% Versawhip or egg white powder.

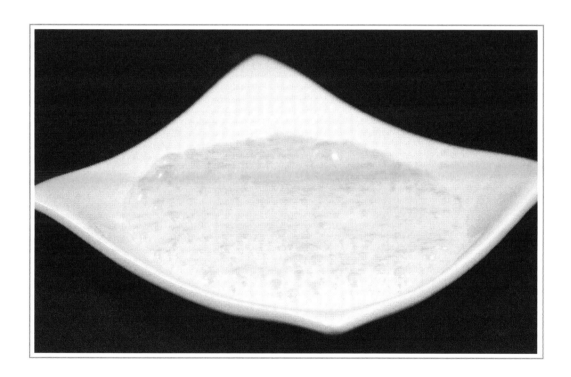

RASPBERRY MINT FOAM

During summer our raspberry bushes overwhelm us with fresh raspberries so I'm always looking for ways to use them up. This raspberry foam is dense, wet, and packs a big flavor punch. It is great on desserts like ice cream or chocolate cake, as a fancy salad dressing, or even to dress fish or chicken.

Since the sweetness of raspberries can vary so much you may need to add more or less honey to balance the flavors. You can also add some vinegar, I prefer champagne or balsamic, if it is too sweet.

You can foam the raspberry puree with an immersion blender but for best results you should use a whipping siphon.

Tools Needed
Xanthan gum
Standing or immersion blender
Whipping siphon (optional)
Strainer
A scale with small gram measurements

Ingredients
200 grams raspberries
1 tablespoon coarsely chopped mint leaves
40 grams honey, about 2 tablespoons
150 grams water
1.5 grams xanthan gum, 0.4%

Combine the raspberries, mint, honey, and water in a blender. Puree until smooth.

If you want a more refined foam, or if you will be using a whipping siphon, strain the puree to remove the raspberry seeds. Return the liquid to the blender.

While blending sprinkle in the xanthan gum and mix until evenly dispersed.

Foam the liquid using a blender, immersion blender, or whipping siphon. For a detailed look at the foaming techniques please see the chapter on Foams.

CUBAN MOJO SAUCE FOAM

This recipes shows how easy it is to take sauces and turn them into light foams. It uses the same recipe from above but increases the xanthan gum to 0.6% from 0.1%.

Tools Needed

Xanthan gum
Standing or immersion blender
A scale with small gram measurements

Ingredients

40 grams olive oil, about 3 tablespoons
8 cloves garlic, minced
78 grams orange juice, about ⅓ cup
78 grams lime juice, about ⅓ cup
1 teaspoon ground cumin
Salt and pepper
1.2 grams xanthan gum, 0.6%

To prepare the mojo sauce heat the olive oil and garlic in a pan over medium-high heat. Cook until the garlic begins to soften, about 1 minute, then add the orange juice, lime juice and cumin. Bring to a simmer and mix well. Salt and pepper to taste.

Remove from the heat and let cool slightly. Pour into a blender or a container that works well with your immersion blender.

Sprinkle in the xanthan gum and blend well. Foam the liquid using a blender, immersion blender, or whipping siphon. For a detailed look at the foaming techniques please see the chapter on Foams.

Xanthan Gum Emulsions

Because xanthan gum thickens liquids it also helps create more stable emulsions. This can be used to hold traditional vinaigrettes together, create new vinaigrettes using purees, or to use much less oil than you usually would.

Emulsion Process

Strengthening an emulsion with xanthan gum is very easy. First create the emulsion like you usually would. Then blend in a pinch of xanthan gum. It will thicken the liquid slightly and help the emulsion hold for a much longer time.

For an even stronger emulsion you can add some soy lecithin at a ratio of 0.3 to 0.5%.

Emulsion Ratios

The more xanthan gum you add, the stronger the emulsion will be. However, it will also thicken the emulsion, which may or may not be desirable. To start binding an emulsion a ratio of around 0.1% can be used. If you want to also thicken the emulsion you can add as much xanthan gum as you want, up to around 0.8%.

Basil Balsamic Sauce

I love the sweet tang of balsamic vinegar when combined with the herbal flavor of basil. This sauce is very simple to put together and the xanthan gum helps it cling to the food much better.

You can serve this on a wide range of foods. It is great on fish or chicken, and can even hold up to steak. I also love it drizzled over fresh mozzarella and tomatoes as a take on a Caprese salad.

Tools Needed
Xanthan gum
Standing or immersion blender
A scale with small gram measurements

Ingredients
45 grams balsamic vinegar, about 3 tablespoons
½ teaspoon finely minced garlic
⅓ cup fresh basil leaves
107 grams olive oil, about ½ cup
Salt and pepper
0.5 grams xanthan gum, 0.3%
2 tablespoons fresh basil leaves, chopped

Place all of the ingredients except the xanthan gum and the 2 tablespoons of chopped basil leaves into a blender or a container that works well with your immersion blender. Blend and taste for seasonings and make sure the balance of the flavors is good, adding more sugar, vinegar, or salt as needed.

Sprinkle in the xanthan gum and blend well to combine. Taste it for thickness and mouthfeel. If you need it thicker, continue adding xanthan gum and blending well until it has the thickness and mouthfeel you prefer.

Stir in the remaining basil leaves and it is ready to serve.

ASIAN VINAIGRETTE

Vinaigrettes are great ways to add flavors not only to salads but also meat and fish. This Asian vinaigrette is awesome on a salad with peanuts and orange wedges but it is equally good on seared tuna or chicken.

Tools Needed
Xanthan gum
Standing or immersion blender
A scale with small gram measurements

Ingredients
15 grams rice wine vinegar, about 1 tablespoon
30 grams fresh orange juice, about 2 tablespoons
15 grams soy sauce, about 1 tablespoon
5 grams fresh ginger, minced or grated on a
    microplane
Salt and pepper

13 grams sesame oil, about 1 tablespoon
55 grams olive oil, about ¼ cup
0.4 grams xanthan gum

Combine the vinegar, orange juice, ginger, soy sauce, salt, and pepper in a small bowl or mixing container. Let sit for 5 minutes. Blend in the oils with an immersion blender or whisk attachment.

Taste the vinaigrette for seasoning and adjust the olive oil and vinegar to control the acidity.

Once the vinaigrette tastes balanced to you add the xanthan gum and blend well to combine. Taste the vinaigrette and make sure the mouthfeel and thickness is what you prefer. Add more xanthan gum or vinegar to adjust the thickness.

The vinaigrette can now be served at any time or can be held for several hours. If holding for longer than a few hours you can refrigerate for a day or two before it breaks.

OTHER INGREDIENTS

We are always adding more ingredients to our modernist glossary. Come by and see what we've been using lately.

You can find it on our website at:
www.modernistcookingmadeeasy.com/info/
molecular-gastronomy-glossary

Because of the large number of ingredients used in modernist cooking we are unable to cover all of them in depth. We picked out the ones we felt were the most useful for beginners but here are some of the other commonly used ones.

CALCIUM CHLORIDE

Calcium chloride is a popular calcium salt and is often used to introduce calcium into mixtures. It is typically used with sodium alginate and other ingredients that require calcium.

Calcium chloride has a harsh, bitter taste so it is not suitable for use in reverse spherification or other methods where it would end up in the final dish.

CALCIUM LACTATE

Calcium lactate is a calcium salt and is one of the most common ways to introduce calcium into mixtures. It is typically used with sodium alginate and other ingredients that require calcium.

Calcium lactate has a mild taste and can be used in both direct and reverse spherification.

CALCIUM SALTS

Other Names
Calcium Lactate, Calcium Gluconate, Calcium Sulfate, Calcium Chloride

Several modernist ingredients, such as sodium alginate, require calcium in the mixture in order to gel or hydrate. If the mixture does not have calcium it can be added through calcium salts.

GELLAN

Common Names
Low Acyl Gellan, High Acyl Gellan

Basic Ratios by Weight
0.5-1.25% for gels

Gellan is a popular gelling agent and comes in two varieties, high acyl or low acyl. High acyl gellan typically results in soft, elastic gels while low acyl gellan creates hard, brittle gels. They are often used together to create a variety of textures. They can also be used in spherification.

The gels created by gellan are highly dependent on the presence of calcium and potassium in the mixture. Gellan must also be heated to hydrate though it sets at high temperatures as well.

GLUCOSE

Glucose is a form of sugar that prevents the formation of crystals when cooked. It is similar to corn syrup and may be substituted as such in most recipes.

GUAR GUM

Common Names
Guarzoon

Basic Ratios by Weight
0.1-1.25% for thickening

Guar gum is one of several gums used in modernist cooking. It is made from the guar bean plant, typically from India.

It has properties similar to xanthan gum, including thickening and emulsifying ingredients as well as retaining water and preventing syneresis. It is also often used in ice creams to prevent crystal formation.

It is soluble in hot or cold water, but has a longer hydration time in cold water. It also works better with neutral to slightly acidic liquids. It is often used with other ingredients such as agar and xanthan gum. If too much is used it can add the flavor of dried beans to the dish.

GUM ARABIC

Basic Ratios By Weight
1.0-45.0% for stabilization and thickening

Gum arabic is made from the Acacia tree's resin. It has been used for thousands of years and can be used to stabilize emulsions and foams.

It can be hydrated in hot or cold liquids by blending.

ISOMALT

Isomalt is a sugar alcohol often used as a sugar substitute and has only half the calories of sugar. It tends to be clear when cooked below 190ºC / 373ºF instead of coloring like sugar does. When clarity is not an issue you can substitute it with regular sugar.

KONJAC

Common Names
Konjac Flour, Konjac Mannan

Basic Ratios by Weight
0.3-1.25% for thickening

Konjac flour is made from the tuber of the konjac plant. It is a gum that can thicken liquids and stabilize emulsions. It can also

gel in alkaline mixtures. It is often combined with other ingredients to improve their thickening and gelling.

It has been used in Japanese cooking for centuries and is used to make noodles as well as puddings and pastes. It is also unusual in the fact that it thickens at high temperatures instead of low ones.

LOCUST BEAN GUM

Common Names
St. John's Bread

Basic Ratios by Weight
0.1-0.3% - fruit filling stabilization

0.1-0.75% typically with other ingredients

Locust bean gum is taken from the seeds of the Mediterranean carob or locust bean tree. It is good at thickening liquids and stabilizing emulsions. It can be used by itself but is more often used to complement other ingredients.

It combines well with ingredients that make brittle gels and strengthens them by making them more elastic. This makes it ideal to use with xanthan gum, kappa and lambda carrageenan, and agar. It can also be used to help keep fruit fillings for pies from boiling out.

Locust bean gum can be dispersed in cold water with a blender and is hydrated in water above 90°C / 194°F. Once hydrated it is typically effective at temperatures below 85°C / 185°F.

Quick Recipe: Elastic Agar Gel

Take 200 grams of flavored liquid and disperse 0.5 grams locust bean gum and 0.4 grams agar into it using an immersion or standing blender.

Bring it to a boil and let it simmer for 3 to 5 minutes. Remove it from the heat and pour into molds. Let cool. You can now turn out the gel, cut it into any shapes you like, and serve.

MONO AND DIGLYCERIDES

Common Names

Glycerin Flakes, Texturas Glice

Basic Ratios By Weight

0.5-2% emulsifying
2-10% thickening

Mono and diglycerides are commonly used to stabilize emulsions and to thicken or foam oils. Unlike many ingredients, they have to be dissolved in oil, not in water.

They are high stability emulsifiers composed of monoglyceride and diglyceride taken from the fats of glycerin and fatty acids. Despite commonly being called "glycerin flakes", they do not actually contain any glycerin.

In order to disperse the mono and diglycerides you have to heat the oil above 60°C / 140°F, at which point they melt and can easily be stirred in.

Quick Recipe: Sesame Oil Foam

Combine 215 grams of sesame oil with 16 grams of mono and diglycerides. Heat the oil until the mono and diglycerides melt. Remove from the heat and let cool to room temperature. Pour into a heat resistant whipping siphon and charge as instructed by the manufacturer. The foam is then ready to be dispensed.

PECTIN

Common Names

High-Methoxyl Pectin (HM Pectin), Low-Methoxyl Pectin (LM Pectin)

Basic Ratios by Weight

0.3-1.0% for HM pectin

0.5-3.0% for LM pectin

Pectin has long been used in the United States to make jams and jellies. It comes in two varieties, high-methoxyl and low-methoxyl. HM Pectin works best with low pH ingredients while LM pectin is commonly used with high pH ingredients, especially to make jellies and jams.

Either pectin can be dispersed in cold water by blending, then heated until it dissolves. The liquid is then cooled and the pectin will gel. HM pectin must be in acidic liquids with high sugar concentrations. LM pectin requires the presence of calcium to gel.

PURE-COTE B790

Basic Ratios by Weight

10-15% for films

Pure-Cote B790 is often used to create clear, flexible films and glasses from liquids. It can be dispersed at hot or cold temperatures and sets quickly at room temperature.

Quick Recipe: Flavored Glass

Take 200 grams of a flavored liquid, place in a blender, and blend in 24 grams Pure-Cote B790. Take a large spoonful of the liquid and pour it onto an acetate sheet, evenly coating it.

Leave the sheet out to dry at room temperature for several hours, or preferably overnight. Once it has dried you can take pieces of the "glass" and use them as garnishes on dishes.

For an even crisper texture you can dehydrate the dried pieces of glass for several hours.

SODIUM CITRATE

Sodium citrate is a common sequestrant used to delay gelling by tying up calcium ions in a liquid. It is only effective at high pH levels.

SODIUM HEXAMETAPHOSPHATE

Sodium hexametaphosphate is commonly used as a sequestrant to tie up calcium ions in solutions to reduce the hydration temperature and delay gelling. Its bland flavor leaves the flavor of the dish unchanged. It can also be used on acidic liquids.

TRIMOLINE

Trimoline is an inverted sugar syrup which helps to control the formation of sugar crystals. Honey is also similar to inverted sugar syrups and can be substituted in many cases.

ULTRA-SPERSE

Common Names
Ultra-Sperse 3, Ultra-Sperse M

Basic Ratios by Weight
0.2-5% for thickening

Ultra-Sperse is a modified tapioca starch and is used in many of the same ways xanthan gum is used. It is very good at thickening liquids and can be dispersed in hot or cold liquids.

Quick Recipe: Fast Gravy
Take 300 grams of good, fresh stock and blend 15 grams of Ultra-Sperse 3 into it. Heat to the serving temperature and serve.

ULTRA-TEX

Common Names
Ultra-Tex 3, Ultra-Tex 4, Ultra-Tex 8

Basic Ratios by Weight
1.0-4.0% for basic thickening

5.0-8.0% for major thickening

Ultra-tex is very similar in use to xanthan gum. It can thicken liquids at most temperatures and often has a better mouthfeel than xanthan gum does at higher concentrations.

VERSAWHIP

Common Names
Versawhip 600, Versawhip 600K

Basic Ratios by Weight

0.5-2.0% for foams with 0.1-0.2% xanthan gum

Versawhip is a soy protein that is used similarly to egg whites or gelatin in the stabilization of foams, especially whipped ones. It has greater strength than egg whites and a greater temperature range than gelatin. However, Versawhip will not work with products containing fat.

It is also often combined with xanthan gum for more stable foams.

Quick Recipe: Flavored Foam

Take 300 grams of a flavored liquid such as fruit juice. Place it in a blender, form a vortex and blend in 3.75 grams Versawhip 600 and 0.45 grams xanthan gum.

Pour into the bowl of a stand mixer fitted with a whisk attachment. Whisk until soft peaks form, 3 to 10 minutes. The foam is then ready to be used. It can also be stored in the refrigerator for several days and re-whipped as needed.

SECTION FOUR

REFERENCES

INGREDIENT TABLES

Ingredient Techniques

X = In main chapter, + in Other Ingredients Section, - Not included

Ingredient	Emulsions	Foams	Gels	Spherification	Thickening
Agar		X	X		
Carrageenan: Iota			X	-	X
Carrageenan: Lambda	-	-			-
Carrageenan: Kappa			X		
Gelatin		X	X		
Gellan	+	+	+		
Guar Gum	+				+
Gum Arabic	+	-			+
Konjac	+		-		+
Lecithin	X	X			
Locust Bean Gum			+		+
Maltodextrin					X
Methylcellulose	-	X	X		
Mono and Diglycerides	X				X
Pectin	-	-	+		
Pure Cote B790			+		
Sodium Alginate			-	X	
Ultra-Sperse	+	+			+
Ultra-Tex	+	+			+
Versawhip		+			
Xanthan Gum	X	X			X

Ingredient Temperatures

When you are trying to determine which ingredient to use, the hydration, setting, and melting temperatures can be very important.

Ingredient	Dispersion	Hydration	Gel Sets	Gel Melts
Agar	Any	100°C / 212°F	40-45°C / 104-113°F	80°C / 175°F
Carrageenan: Iota	Cool	Above 70°C / 158°F	40-70°C / 104-158°F	5-10°C / 9-18°F above setting
Carrageenan: Kappa	Cool	Above 70°C / 158°F	35-60°C / 95-140°F	10-20°C / 18-36°F above setting
Gelatin	Above 50°C / 122°F	Cool	30°C / 86°F	30°C / 86°F - 40°C / 104°F
Lecithin	Any	Any	N/A	N/A
Maltodextrin	Room temperature	N/A	N/A	N/A
Methylcellulose				
Methocel F50	Any	Below 15°C / 59°F	Above 62-68°C / 143-154°F	Below 30°C / 86°F
Methocel A4C	Hot	Below 15°C / 59°F	Above 50-55°C / 122-131°F	Below 25°C / 77°F
Mono and Diglycerides	Above 60°C / 140°F	Any	N/A	N/A
Sodium Alginate	Any	Any	Any	Above 130°C / 266°F
Xanthan Gum	Any	Any	N/A	N/A

Sous Vide Time and Temperature

You can also get this time and temperature information
on your mobile phone if you have an iPhone, iPad or an Android.

Just search for "Sous Vide" and look for the guide by "Primolicious".

One of the most interesting aspects of sous vide cooking is how much the time and temperature used can change the texture of the food. Many people experiment with different cooking times and temperatures to tweak dishes various ways.

The numbers below are merely beginning recommendations and are a good place to start. Feel free to increase or lower the temperature several degrees or play around with the cooking time as you see fit as long as you stay in the safe-zone.

DONENESS RANGE

One of the most common questions we get asked about our sous vide recipes is some variation of "the recipe says to cook it for 3 to 6 hours, but when is it actually done".

The short answer is that anytime within the given range the food is "done". As long as the food has been in the water bath for more than the minimum time and less than the maximum time, then it is done. There isn't a specific magical moment of true doneness that can be generalized.

For those that want more information, here's the explanation why.

The How and Why

To have this conversation we first need to determine what "done" actually means. For sous vide there are two main "doneness" concerns when cooking your food. The first is to ensure that the food actually comes up to the temperature you are cooking it at (or becomes pasteurized at for some food). The second concern is making sure the food is tender enough to eat without being "over tender", mushy, or dry.

Once the food you are cooking is completely up to temperature and it is tenderized enough to eat (and not over tenderized), it is now "done". For some already tender cuts of meat like filets, loins, and chicken breasts you don't have to worry about tenderness since they start out that way. That means that these cuts are "done" once they get up to temperature. You can find out this time using our Sous Vide Thickness Ruler.

However, despite them being "done" at the minimum time shown, they stay "done" for several hours past that time, depending on the starting tenderness of the meat. This is why we give a range. You can eat a 1" cut of filet mignon after 50 minutes but you can also eat the filet up to 3 hours after it has gone into the bath without any loss in quality, tenderness, or flavor.

This is how our ranges are determined. They specify that for an average cut of the given meat, they will become "great to eat" tender at the minimum time given. They will continue to get more tender the longer they are in the bath but will remain "great to eat" tender until the final time given, at which point they may begin to get mushy and overcooked. In essence, they will be "done", and very tasty, for that entire span between the minimum and maximum times.

Another Way to Look at It

Another way to think about how this works is to use the following analogy. Pretend you were helping a new cook grill a steak. If they told you they wanted to cook it medium rare and asked you to tell them how to tell when it was "done", what would you say?

Most people would reply with "when the temperature is between 131°F to 139°F".

If the friend isn't a cook they would ask "Yeah, but when is it actually done?"

The answer at this point really comes down to personal preference since to some people medium rare is perfect at 131°F and others prefer a little more well-done 135°F, but a medium rare steak is "done" anywhere in that range.

Other Critical Variables

One other complicating factor is that there are many variables that go into determining how fast a piece of meat tenderizes and/or becomes tender.

The most obvious variable is that some cuts of meat are tougher than others. For example, a top round roast needs to be tenderized a lot longer than a ribeye. Most people realize this and that's why almost all sous vide charts break the food down by "cut".

Another less obvious but almost as important factor is where the meat came from. There is a big difference between how fast the meat tenderizes and how the cow was raised. I've found that grass-fed meat from my local farmer needs just 1/2 the time to become tender compared to supermarket meat (this is also true when roasting or braising them). I've also talked to a reader in Mexico who eats local grass-fed beef that needs slightly longer times than normal because the cows work more.

There are then the variables in the actual cow itself. Whether the meat is prime, choice, etc. makes a difference in tenderizing time. As does the marbling, how old the meat is, and several other factors.

So taking all of this together it can be hard to accurately determine a range of "doneness" that will work for all cuts of meat. But we try our best to come up with a nice range of times that the "average" piece of meat will be done in. The only way to really learn is to experiment with the types of meat in your area and see how they react. And luckily for us, sous vide allows us to have a wide range that food is done in.

In Conclusion

So while there might be one magical moment in the cooking process where a certain piece of meat is the most ideal tenderness, in practice there is a wide time range in the cooking process where the meat will be "done". As long as you take it out sometime in that range it should turn out great.

As you get more experience with your local meats, and determine your personal preferences, you can start to tweak your cook times to suit them more exactly. But as you are learning just remember that the food will be "done" anywhere in that range, and don't sweat the details!

Beef - Roasts and Tough Cuts

Bottom Round Roast
Medium Rare	131°F for 2 to 3 Days (55.0°C)
Medium	140°F for 2 to 3 Days (60.0°C)
Well-Traditional	160°F for 1 to 2 Days (71.1°C)

Brisket
Medium Rare	131°F for 2 to 3 Days (55.0°C)
Medium	140°F for 2 to 3 Days (60.0°C)
Well-Traditional	160°F for 1 to 2 Days (71.1°C)

Cheek
Medium Rare	131°F for 2 to 3 Days (55.0°C)
Medium	149°F for 2 to 3 Days (65.0°C)
Well-Traditional	160°F for 1 to 2 Days (71.1°C)

Chuck Roast
Medium Rare	131°F for 2 to 3 Days (55.0°C)
Medium	140°F for 2 to 3 Days (60.0°C)
Well-Traditional	160°F for 1 to 2 Days (71.1°C)

Pot Roast
Medium Rare	131°F for 2 to 3 Days (55.0°C)
Medium	140°F for 2 to 3 Days (60.0°C)
Well-Traditional	160°F for 1 to 2 Days (71.1°C)

Prime Rib Roast
Medium Rare	131°F for 5 to 10 Hours (55°C)
Medium	140°F for 5 to 10 Hours (60°C)

Rib Eye Roast
Medium Rare	131°F for 5 to 10 Hours (55°C)
Medium	140°F for 5 to 10 Hours (60°C)

Ribs
Medium Rare	131°F for 2 to 3 Days (55.0°C)
Medium	140°F for 2 to 3 Days (60.0°C)
Well-Traditional	160°F for 1 to 2 Days (71.1°C)

Shank
Medium Rare	131°F for 2 to 3 Days (55.0°C)
Medium	140°F for 2 to 3 Days (60.0°C)
Well-Traditional	160°F for 1 to 2 Days (71.1°C)

Short Ribs
Medium Rare	131°F for 2 to 3 Days (55.0°C)
Medium	140°F for 2 to 3 Days (60.0°C)
Well-Traditional	160°F for 1 to 2 Days (71.1°C)

Sirloin Roast
Medium Rare	131°F for 5 to 10 Hours (55.0°C)
Medium	140°F for 5 to 10 Hours (60.0°C)

Stew Meat
Medium Rare	131°F for 4 to 8 Hours (55.0°C)
Medium	140°F for 4 to 8 Hours (60.0°C)

Sweetbreads
Medium	140°F for 30 to 45 Min (60°C)
Pre-Roasting	152°F for 60 Min (66.7°C)

Tenderloin Roast
Medium Rare	131°F for 3 to 6 Hours (55.0°C)
Medium	140°F for 3 to 6 Hours (60.0°C)

Tongue
Low and Slow	140°F for 48 Hours (60.0°C)
High and Fast	158°F for 24 Hours (70.0°C)

Top Loin Strip Roast
Medium Rare	131°F for 4 to 8 Hours (55.0°C)
Medium	140°F for 4 to 8 Hours (60.0°C)

Top Round Roast
Medium Rare	131°F for 1 to 3 Days (55.0°C)
Medium	140°F for 1 to 3 Days (60.0°C)
Well-Traditional	160°F for 1 to 2 Days (71.1°C)

Tri-Tip Roast
Medium Rare	131°F for 5 to 10 Hours (55°C)
Medium	140°F for 5 to 10 Hours (60°C)

Beef - Steak and Tender Cuts

Blade Steak
Medium Rare   131°F for 4 to 10 Hours (55.0°C)
Medium   140°F for 4 to 10 Hours (60.0°C)

Bottom Round Steak
Medium Rare   131°F for 1 to 3 Days (55.0°C)
Medium   140°F for 1 to 3 Days (60.0°C)

Chuck Steak
Medium Rare   131°F for 1 to 2 Days (55.0°C)
Medium   140°F for 1 to 2 Days (60.0°C)

Eye Round Steak
Medium Rare   131°F for 1 to 2 Days (55.0°C)
Medium   140°F for 1 to 2 Days (60.0°C)

Flank Steak
Medium Rare   131°F for 2 to 12 Hours (55.0°C)
Medium Rare and Tender   131°F for 1 to 2 Days (55.0°C)
Medium   140°F for 2 to 12 Hours (60.0°C)
Medium and Tender   140°F for 1 to 2 Days (60.0°C)

Flat Iron Steak
Medium Rare   131°F for 4 to 10 Hours (55.0°C)
Medium   140°F for 4 to 10 Hours (60.0°C)

Hamburger
Medium Rare   131°F for 2 to 4 Hours (55.0°C)
Medium   140°F for 2 to 4 Hours (60.0°C)

Hanger Steak
Medium Rare   131°F for 2 to 3 Hours (55.0°C)
Medium   140°F for 2 to 3 Hours (60.0°C)

Porterhouse Steak
Medium Rare   131°F for 2 to 3 Hours (55.0°C)
Medium   140°F for 2 to 3 Hours (60.0°C)

Rib Steak
Medium Rare   131°F for 2 to 8 Hours (55.0°C)
Medium   140°F for 2 to 8 Hours (60.0°C)

Ribeye Steak
Medium Rare   131°F for 2 to 8 Hours (55.0°C)
Medium   140°F for 2 to 8 Hours (60.0°C)

Sausage
Medium Rare   131°F for 2 to 3 Hours (55.0°C)
Medium   140°F for 90 to 120 Min (60°C)

Shoulder Steak
Medium Rare   131°F for 4 to 10 Hours (55.0°C)
Medium   140°F for 4 to 10 Hours (60.0°C)

Sirloin Steak
Medium Rare   131°F for 2 to 10 Hours (55.0°C)
Medium   140°F for 2 to 10 Hours (60.0°C)

Skirt Steak
Medium Rare   131°F for 1 to 2 Days (55.0°C)
Medium   140°F for 1 to 2 Days (60.0°C)

T-Bone Steak
Medium Rare   131°F for 2 to 3 Hours (55.0°C)
Medium   140°F for 2 to 3 Hours (60.0°C)

Tenderloin Steak
Medium Rare   131°F for 2 to 3 Hours (55.0°C)
Medium   140°F for 2 to 3 Hours (60.0°C)

Top Loin Strip Steak
Medium Rare   131°F for 2 to 3 Hours (55.0°C)
Medium   140°F for 2 to 3 Hours (60.0°C)

Top Round Steak
Medium Rare   131°F for 1 to 2 Days (55.0°C)
Medium   140°F for 1 to 2 Days (60.0°C)

Tri-Tip Steak
Medium Rare   131°F for 2 to 10 Hours (55.0°C)
Medium   140°F for 2 to 10 Hours (60.0°C)

CHICKEN AND EGGS

Breast

Rare	136°F for 1 to 4 Hours (57.8°C)
Medium / Typical	140°F - 147°F for 1 to 4 Hours (63.9°C)
More Dry	140°F - 147°F for 4 to 12 Hours (63.9°C)

Drumstick

Rare	140°F for 90 to 120 Min (60.0°C)
Ideal	148°F - 156°F for 2 to 5 Hours (64.4°C)
For Shredding	160°F - 170°F for 8 to 12 Hours (71.1°C)

Eggs

Over Easy	142°F - 146°F for 45 to 60 Min (62.8°C)
Poached	142°F for 45 to 60 Min (61.1°C)
Perfect	148°F for 45 to 60 Min (64.4°C)
Hard Boiled	149°F - 152°F for 45 to 60 Min (65.6°C)
Pasteurized	135°F for 75 Min (57.2°C)

Leg

Rare	140°F for 90 to 120 Min (60.0°C)
Ideal	148°F - 156°F for 2 to 5 Hours (64.4°C)
For Shredding	160°F - 170°F for 8 to 12 Hours (71.1°C)

Sausage

White Meat	140°F for 1 to 2 Hours (63.9°C)
Mixed Meat	140°F for 90 to 120 Min (60.0°C)

Thigh

Rare	140°F for 90 to 120 Min (60.0°C)
Ideal	148°F - 156°F for 2 to 5 Hours (64.4°C)
For Shredding	160°F - 170°F for 8 to 12 Hours (71.1°C)

Whole Chicken

Rare	140°F for 4 to 6 Hours (60.0°C)
Typical	148°F for 4 to 6 Hours (64.4°C)
Larger	148°F for 6 to 8 Hours (64.4°C)
Butterflied	148°F for 2 to 4 Hours (64.4°C)

DUCK

Breast
Medium Rare	131°F for 2 to 4 Hours (55.0°C)
Medium	140°F for 2 to 4 Hours (60.0°C)

Drumstick
Medium Rare	131°F for 3 to 6 Hours (55.0°C)
Well	176°F for 8 to 10 Hours (80.0°C)
Confit	167°F for 10 to 20 Hours (75.0°C)

Foie Gras
Foie Gras	134°F for 35 to 55 Min (56.7°C)

Leg
Medium Rare	131°F for 3 to 6 Hours (55.0°C)
Well	176°F for 8 to 10 Hours (80.0°C)
Duck Confit	167°F for 10 to 20 Hours (75.0°C)

Sausage
Breast Meat	131°F for 1 to 2 Hours (55.0°C)
Mixed Meat	131°F for 2 to 3 Hours (55.0°C)

Thigh
Medium Rare	131°F for 3 to 6 Hours (55.0°C)
Well	176°F for 8 to 10 Hours (80.0°C)
Confit	167°F for 10 to 20 Hours (75.0°C)

Whole Duck
Medium Rare	131°F for 3 to 6 Hours (55.0°C)
Medium	140°F for 3 to 6 Hours (60.0°C)
Confit	167°F for 10 to 20 Hours (75.0°C)

FISH AND SHELLFISH

Arctic Char

"Sushi", Rare	104°F for 10 to 30 Min (40.0°C)
"Sushi", Medium Rare	122°F for 10 to 30 Min (50.0°C)
Medium Rare	132°F for 10 to 30 Min (55.6°C)
Medium	140°F for 10 to 30 Min (60.0°C)

Bass

"Sushi", Rare	104°F for 10 to 30 Min (40.0°C)
"Sushi", Medium Rare	122°F for 10 to 30 Min (50.0°C)
Medium Rare	132°F for 10 to 30 Min (55.6°C)
Medium	140°F for 10 to 30 Min (60.0°C)

Black Sea Bass

"Sushi", Rare	104°F for 10 to 30 Min (40.0°C)
"Sushi", Medium Rare	122°F for 10 to 30 Min (50.0°C)
Medium Rare	132°F for 10 to 30 Min (55.6°C)
Medium	140°F for 10 to 30 Min (60.0°C)

Bluefish

"Sushi", Medium Rare	122°F for 10 to 30 Min (50.0°C)
Medium Rare	132°F for 10 to 30 Min (55.6°C)
Medium	140°F for 10 to 30 Min (60.0°C)

Carp

"Sushi", Medium Rare	122°F for 10 to 30 Min (50.0°C)
Medium Rare	132°F for 10 to 30 Min (55.6°C)
Medium	140°F for 10 to 30 Min (60.0°C)

Catfish

"Sushi", Medium Rare	122°F for 10 to 30 Min (50.0°C)
Medium Rare	132°F for 10 to 30 Min (55.6°C)
Medium	140°F for 10 to 30 Min (60.0°C)

Cod

Rare	104°F for 10 to 30 Min (40.0°C)
"Sushi", Medium Rare	129°F for 10 to 30 Min (53.9°C)
Medium Rare	132°F for 10 to 30 Min (55.6°C)

Flounder

"Sushi", Medium Rare	122°F for 10 to 30 Min (50.0°C)
Medium Rare	132°F for 10 to 30 Min (55.6°C)
Medium	140°F for 10 to 30 Min (60.0°C)

Grouper

"Sushi", Rare	104°F for 10 to 30 Min (40.0°C)
"Sushi", Medium Rare	122°F for 10 to 30 Min (50.0°C)
Medium Rare	132°F for 10 to 30 Min (55.6°C)
Medium	140°F for 10 to 30 Min (60.0°C)

Haddock

"Sushi", Medium Rare	122°F for 10 to 30 Min (50.0°C)
Medium Rare	132°F for 10 to 30 Min (55.6°C)
Medium	140°F for 10 to 30 Min (60.0°C)

Hake

"Sushi", Rare	104°F for 10 to 30 Min (40.0°C)
"Sushi", Medium Rare	122°F for 10 to 30 Min (50.0°C)
Medium Rare	132°F for 10 to 30 Min (55.6°C)
Medium	140°F for 10 to 30 Min (60.0°C)

Halibut

"Sushi", Rare	104°F for 10 to 30 Min (40.0°C)
"Sushi", Medium Rare	129°F for 10 to 30 Min (53.9°C)
Medium Rare	132°F for 10 to 30 Min (55.6°C)
Medium	140°F for 10 to 30 Min (60.0°C)

King Crab Tail

King Crab Tail	140°F for 30 to 45 Min (60.0°C)

Lobster

Medium Rare	126°F for 15 to 40 Min (52.2°C)
Medium	140°F for 15 to 40 Min (60.0°C)

Mackerel

"Sushi", Rare	109°F for 10 to 30 Min (42.8°C)
"Sushi", Medium Rare	122°F for 10 to 30 Min (50.0°C)
Medium Rare	132°F for 10 to 30 Min (55.6°C)

Mahi Mahi

"Sushi", Medium Rare	122°F for 10 to 30 Min (50.0°C)
Medium Rare	132°F for 10 to 30 Min (55.6°C)
Medium	140°F for 10 to 30 Min (60.0°C)

Marlin

"Sushi", Rare	104°F for 10 to 30 Min (40.0°C)
"Sushi", Medium Rare	122°F for 10 to 30 Min (50.0°C)
Medium Rare	132°F for 10 to 30 Min (55.6°C)
Medium	140°F for 10 to 30 Min (60.0°C)

Monkfish

"Sushi", Rare	104°F for 10 to 30 Min (40.0°C)
"Sushi", Medium Rare	118°F for 10 to 30 Min (47.8°C)
Medium Rare	132°F for 10 to 30 Min (55.6°C)
Medium	140°F for 10 to 30 Min (60.0°C)

Octopus

Slow Cook	170°F for 4 to 7 Hours (76.7°C)
Fast Cook	180°F for 2 to 3 Hours (82.2°C)

Red Snapper

"Sushi", Rare	104°F for 10 to 30 Min (40.0°C)
"Sushi", Medium Rare	122°F for 10 to 30 Min (50.0°C)
Medium Rare	132°F for 10 to 30 Min (55.6°C)
Medium	140°F for 10 to 30 Min (60.0°C)

Salmon

"Sushi", Rare	104°F for 10 to 30 Min (40.0°C)
"Sushi", Medium Rare	122°F for 10 to 30 Min (50.0°C)
Medium Rare	132°F for 10 to 30 Min (55.6°C)
Medium	140°F for 10 to 30 Min (60.0°C)

Sardines

"Sushi", Rare	104°F for 10 to 30 Min (40.0°C)
"Sushi", Medium Rare	122°F for 10 to 30 Min (50.0°C)
Medium Rare	132°F for 10 to 30 Min (55.6°C)
Medium	140°F for 10 to 30 Min (60.0°C)

Scallops

Pre-Sear	122°F for 15 to 35 Min (50.0°C)

Scrod

"Sushi", Medium Rare	122°F for 10 to 30 Min (50.0°C)
Medium Rare	132°F for 10 to 30 Min (55.6°C)
Medium	140°F for 10 to 30 Min (60.0°C)

Sea Bass

"Sushi", Rare	104°F for 10 to 30 Min (40.0°C)
"Sushi", Medium Rare	122°F for 10 to 30 Min (50.0°C)
Medium Rare	132°F for 10 to 30 Min (55.6°C)
Medium	140°F for 10 to 30 Min (60.0°C)

Shark

"Sushi", Medium Rare	122°F for 10 to 30 Min (50.0°C)
Medium Rare	132°F for 10 to 30 Min (55.6°C)
Medium	140°F for 10 to 30 Min (60.0°C)

Shrimp

"Sushi" Medium Rare	122°F for 15 to 35 Min (50.0°C)
Medium Rare	132°F for 15 to 35 Min (55.6°C)

Skate

"Sushi", Medium Rare	129°F for 10 to 30 Min (53.9°C)
Medium Rare	132°F for 10 to 30 Min (55.6°C)
Medium	140°F for 10 to 30 Min (60.0°C)

Soft Shell Crab

Standard	145°F for 3 hours (62.8°C)

Sole

"Sushi", Medium Rare	122°F for 10 to 30 Min (50.0°C)
Medium Rare	132°F for 10 to 30 Min (55.6°C)
Medium	143°F for 10 to 30 Min (61.7°C)

Squid

Pre-Sear	113°F for 45 to 60 Min (45.0°C)
Low Heat	138°F for 2 to 4 Hours (58.9°C)
High Heat	180°F for 1 Hour (82.2°C)

Striped Bass

"Sushi", Rare	104°F for 10 to 30 Min (40.0°C)
"Sushi", Medium Rare	122°F for 10 to 30 Min (50.0°C)
Medium Rare	132°F for 10 to 30 Min (55.6°C)
Medium	140°F for 10 to 30 Min (60.0°C)

Sturgeon

"Sushi", Rare	104°F for 10 to 30 Min (40.0°C)
"Sushi", Medium Rare	122°F for 10 to 30 Min (50.0°C)
Medium Rare	132°F for 10 to 30 Min (55.6°C)
Medium	140°F for 10 to 30 Min (60.0°C)

Swordfish

"Sushi", Rare	104°F for 10 to 30 Min (40.0°C)
"Sushi", Medium Rare	122°F for 10 to 30 Min (50.0°C)
Medium Rare	132°F for 10 to 30 Min (55.6°C)
Medium	140°F for 10 to 30 Min (60.0°C)

Tilapia

"Sushi", Rare	104°F for 10 to 30 Min (40.0°C)
"Sushi", Medium Rare	122°F for 10 to 30 Min (50.0°C)
Medium Rare	132°F for 10 to 30 Min (55.6°C)
Medium	140°F for 10 to 30 Min (60.0°C)

Trout

"Sushi", Medium Rare	122°F for 10 to 30 Min (50.0°C)
Medium Rare	132°F for 10 to 30 Min (55.6°C)
Medium	140°F for 10 to 30 Min (60.0°C)

Tuna

"Sushi", Rare	100°F for 10 to 20 Min (37.8°C)
"Sushi", Medium Rare	129°F for 10 to 30 Min (53.9°C)
Medium Rare	132°F for 10 to 30 Min (55.6°C)

Turbot

"Sushi", Medium Rare	129°F for 10 to 30 Min (53.9°C)
Medium Rare	132°F for 10 to 30 Min (55.6°C)
Medium	140°F for 10 to 30 Min (60.0°C)

FRUITS AND VEGETABLES

Acorn Squash	183°F for 1 to 2 Hours (83.9°C)
Apples	183°F for 25 to 40 Min (83.9°C)
Artichokes	183°F for 45 to 75 Min (83.9°C)
Asparagus	183°F for 30 to 40 Min (83.9°C)
Banana	183°F for 10 to 15 Min (83.9°C)
Beet	183°F for 30 to 60 Min (83.9°C)
Broccoli	183°F for 20 to 30 Min (83.9°C)
Brussels Sprouts	183°F for 45 to 60 Min (83.9°C)
Butternut Squash	183°F for 1 to 2 Hours (83.9°C)
Cabbage	183°F for 30 to 45 Min (83.9°C)
Carrot	183°F for 40 to 60 Min (83.9°C)
Cauliflower	
Florets	183°F for 20 to 30 Min (83.9°C)
For Puree	183°F for 2 Hours (83.9°C)
Stems	183°F for 60 to 75 Min (83.9°C)
Celery Root	183°F for 60 to 75 Min (83.9°C)
Chard	183°F for 60 to 75 Min (83.9°C)
Cherries	183°F for 15 to 25 Min (83.9°C)
Corn	183°F for 30 to 45 Min (83.9°C)
Eggplant	183°F for 30 to 45 Min (83.9°C)
Fennel	183°F for 40 to 60 Min (83.9°C)
Golden Beets	183°F for 30 to 60 Min (83.9°C)
Green Beans	183°F for 30 to 45 Min (83.9°C)
Leek	183°F for 30 to 60 Min (83.9°C)
Onion	183°F for 35 to 45 Min (83.9°C)
Parsnip	183°F for 30 to 60 Min (83.9°C)
Pea Pods	183°F for 30 to 40 Min (83.9°C)
Peaches	183°F for 30 to 60 Min (83.9°C)

Pears	183°F for 25 to 35 Min (83.9°C)
Pineapple	167°F for 45 to 60 Min (75.0°C)
Plums	167°F for 15 to 20 Min (75.0°C)
Potatoes	
Small	183°F for 30 to 60 Min (83.9°C)
Large	183°F for 60 to 120 Min (83.9°C)
Pumpkin	183°F for 45 to 60 Min (83.9°C)
Radish	183°F for 10 to 25 Min (83.9°C)
Rhubarb	141°F for 25 to 45 Min (60.6°C)
Rutabaga	183°F for 2 Hours (83.9°C)
Salsify	183°F for 45 to 60 Min (83.9°C)
Squash, Summer	183°F for 30 to 60 Min (83.9°C)
Squash, Winter	183°F for 1 to 2 Hours (83.9°C)
Sunchokes	183°F for 40 to 60 Min (83.9°C)
Sweet Potatoes	
Small	183°F for 45 to 60 Min (83.9°C)
Large	183°F for 60 to 90 Min (83.9°C)
Swiss Chard	183°F for 60 to 75 Min (83.9°C)
Turnip	183°F for 30 to 45 Min (83.9°C)
Yams	183°F for 30 to 60 Min (83.9°C)
Zucchini	183°F for 30 to 60 Min (83.9°C)

LAMB

Arm Chop
Medium Rare 131°F for 18 to 36 Hours (55.0°C)
Medium   140°F for 18 to 36 Hours (60.0°C)

Blade Chop
Medium Rare 131°F for 18 to 36 Hours (55.0°C)
Medium   140°F for 18 to 36 Hours (60.0°C)

Breast
Medium Rare   131°F for 20 to 28 Hours (55.0°C)
Medium   140°F for 20 to 28 Hours (60.0°C)
Well-Traditional 165°F for 20 to 28 Hours (73.9°C)

Leg, Bone In
Rare   126°F for 1 to 2 Days (52.2°C)
Medium Rare 131°F for 2 to 3 Days (55.0°C)
Medium   140°F for 1 to 3 Days (60.0°C)

Leg, Boneless
Medium Rare 131°F for 18 to 36 Hours (55.0°C)
Medium   140°F for 18 to 36 Hours (60.0°C)

Loin Chops
Rare   126°F for 1 to 2 Hours (52.2°C)
Medium Rare 131°F for 2 to 4 Hours (55.0°C)
Medium   140°F for 2 to 3 Hours (60.0°C)

Loin Roast
Rare   126°F for 1 to 2 Hours (52.2°C)
Medium Rare 131°F for 2 to 4 Hours (55.0°C)
Medium   140°F for 2 to 3 Hours (60.0°C)

Loin, Boneless
Rare   126°F for 1 to 2 Hours (52.2°C)
Medium Rare 131°F for 2 to 4 Hours (55.0°C)
Medium   140°F for 2 to 3 Hours (60.0°C)

Neck
Medium Rare   131°F for 2 to 3 Days (55.0°C)
Medium   140°F for 2 to 3 Days (60.0°C)
Well-Traditional 165°F for 1 to 2 Days (73.9°C)

Osso Buco
Medium Rare   131°F for 1 to 2 Days (55.0°C)
Medium   140°F for 1 to 2 Days (60.0°C)
Well-Traditional 165°F for 1 to 2 Days (73.9°C)

Rack
Rare   126°F for 1 to 2 Hours (52.2°C)
Medium Rare 131°F for 2 to 3 Hours (55.0°C)
Medium   140°F for 1 to 3 Hours (60.0°C)

Rib Chop
Rare   126°F for 1 to 2 Hours (52.2°C)
Medium Rare 131°F for 2 to 3 Hours (55.0°C)
Medium   140°F for 1 to 3 Hours (60.0°C)

Ribs
Medium Rare   131°F for 22 to 26 Hours (55.0°C)
Medium   140°F for 22 to 26 Hours (60.0°C)
Well-Traditional 165°F for 22 to 26 Hours (73.9°C)

Shank
Medium Rare   131°F for 1 to 2 Days (55.0°C)
Medium   140°F for 1 to 2 Days (60.0°C)
Well-Traditional 165°F for 1 to 2 Days (73.9°C)

Shoulder
Medium Rare   131°F for 1 to 2 Days (55.0°C)
Medium   140°F for 1 to 2 Days (60.0°C)
Well-Traditional 165°F for 18 to 36 Hours (73.9°C)

Tenderloin
Rare   126°F for 1 to 2 Hours (52.2°C)
Medium Rare 131°F for 2 to 3 Hours (55.0°C)
Medium   140°F for 1 to 3 Hours (60.0°C)

PORK

Arm Steak
Medium Rare	131°F for 1 to 2 Days (55.0°C)
Medium	140°F for 1 to 2 Days (60.0°C)

Baby Back Ribs
Medium Rare	131°F for 8 to 10 Hours (55.0°C)
Medium	140°F for 8 to 10 Hours (60.0°C)
Well-Traditional	155°F for 12 to 24 Hours (68.3°C)

Back Ribs
Medium Rare	131°F for 8 to 12 Hours (55.0°C)
Medium	140°F for 8 to 12 Hours (60.0°C)
Well-Traditional	155°F for 12 to 24 Hours (68.3°C)

Belly
Low and Slow	140°F for 2 to 3 Days (60.0°C)
In Between	160°F for 18 to 36 Hours (71.1°C)
High and Fast	180°F for 12 to 18 Hours (82.2°C)

Blade Chops
Medium Rare	131°F for 8 to 12 Hours (55.0°C)
Medium	140°F for 8 to 12 Hours (60.0°C)

Blade Roast
Medium Rare	131°F for 1 to 2 Days (55.0°C)
Medium	140°F for 1 to 2 Days (60.0°C)
Well-Traditional	155°F for 1 to 2 Days (68.3°C)

Blade Steak
Medium Rare	131°F for 18 to 36 Hours (55.0°C)
Medium	140°F for 18 to 36 Hours (60.0°C)

Boston Butt
Medium Rare	131°F for 1 to 2 Days (55.0°C)
Medium	140°F for 1 to 2 Days (60.0°C)
Well-Traditional	155°F for 1 to 2 Days (68.3°C)

Butt Roast
Medium Rare	131°F for 18 to 36 Hours (55.0°C)
Medium	140°F for 18 to 36 Hours (60.0°C)
Well-Traditional	155°F for 18 to 36 Hours (68.3°C)

Country Style Ribs
Medium Rare	131°F for 8 to 12 Hours (55.0°C)
Medium	140°F for 8 to 12 Hours (60.0°C)
Well-Traditional	155°F for 12 to 24 Hours (68.3°C)

Fresh Side Pork
Low and Slow	140°F for 2 to 3 Days (60.0°C)
In Between	160°F for 18 to 36 Hours (71.1°C)
High and Fast	180°F for 12 to 18 Hours (82.2°C)

Ground Pork
Medium Rare	131°F for 2 to 4 Hours (55.0°C)
Medium	140°F for 2 to 4 Hours (60.0°C)

Ham Roast
Medium Rare	131°F for 10 to 20 Hours (55.0°C)
Medium	140°F for 10 to 20 Hours (60.0°C)
Well-Traditional	155°F for 10 to 20 Hours (68.3°C)

Ham Steak
Medium Rare	131°F for 2 to 3 Hours (55.0°C)
Medium	140°F for 2 to 3 Hours (60.0°C)

Kebabs
Medium Rare	131°F for 3 to 8 Hours (55.0°C)
Medium	140°F for 3 to 8 Hours (60.0°C)
Well-Traditional	155°F for 3 to 8 Hours (68.3°C)

Leg (Fresh Ham)
Medium Rare	131°F for 10 to 20 Hours (55.0°C)
Medium	140°F for 10 to 20 Hours (60.0°C)
Well-Traditional	155°F for 10 to 20 Hours (68.3°C)

Loin Chop
Medium Rare	131°F for 3 to 5 Hours (55.0°C)
Medium	140°F for 2 to 4 Hours (60.0°C)

Loin Roast
Medium Rare	131°F for 4 to 8 Hours (55.0°C)
Medium	140°F for 4 to 6 Hours (60.0°C)

Picnic Roast
Medium Rare	131°F for 1 to 3 Days (55.0°C)
Medium	140°F for 1 to 3 Days (60.0°C)
Well-Traditional	155°F for 1 to 3 Days (68.3°C)

Pork Chops
Medium Rare	131°F for 3 to 6 Hours (55.0°C)
Medium	140°F for 2 to 4 Hours (60.0°C)

Rib Chops
Medium Rare	131°F for 5 to 8 Hours (55.0°C)
Medium	140°F for 4 to 7 Hours (60.0°C)

Rib Roast
Medium Rare	131°F for 5 to 8 Hours (55.0°C)
Medium	140°F for 4 to 7 Hours (60.0°C)

Sausage
Medium Rare	131°F for 2 to 3 Hours (55.0°C)
Medium	140°F for 2 to 3 Hours (60.0°C)
Well-Traditional	155°F for 2 to 3 Hours (68.3°C)

Shank
Medium Rare	131°F for 8 to 10 Hours (55.0°C)
Medium	140°F for 8 to 10 Hours (60.0°C)

Shoulder
Medium Rare	135°F for 1 to 2 Days (57.2°C)
Medium	145°F for 1 to 2 Days (62.8°C)
Well-Traditional	155°F for 1 to 2 Days (68.3°C)

Sirloin Chops
Medium Rare	131°F for 6 to 12 Hours (55.0°C)
Medium	140°F for 5 to 10 Hours (60.0°C)

Sirloin Roast
Medium Rare	131°F for 6 to 12 Hours (55.0°C)
Medium	140°F for 5 to 10 Hours (60.0°C)
Well-Traditional	155°F for 10 to 16 Hours (68.3°C)

Spare Ribs
Medium Rare	131°F for 12 to 24 Hours (55.0°C)
Medium	140°F for 12 to 24 Hours (60.0°C)
Well-Traditional	155°F for 12 to 24 Hours (68.3°C)

Spleen
Spleen	145°F for 1 Hour (62.8°C)

Tenderloin
Medium Rare	131°F for 3 to 6 Hours (55.0°C)
Medium	140°F for 2 to 4 Hours (60.0°C)

TURKEY

Breast
"Rare"   136°F for 1 to 4 Hours (57.8°C)
Medium / Typical 140°F - 147°F for 1 to 4 Hours (63.9°C)

Drumstick
Medium Rare   140°F for 3 to 4 Hours (60.0°C)
Ideal   148°F for 4 to 8 Hours (64.4°C)
For Shredding 160°F for 18 to 24 Hours (71.1°C)

Leg
Medium Rare   140°F for 3 to 4 Hours (60.0°C)
Ideal   148°F for 4 to 8 Hours (64.4°C)
For Shredding 160°F for 18 to 24 Hours (71.1°C)

Sausage
White Meat   140°F for 1 to 4 Hours (63.9°C)
Mixed Meat   140°F for 3 to 4 Hours (64.4°C)

Thigh
Medium Rare   140°F for 3 to 4 Hours (60.0°C)
Ideal   148°F for 4 to 8 Hours (64.4°C)
For Shredding 160°F for 18 to 24 Hours (71.1°C)

FAHRENHEIT TO CELSIUS CONVERSION

This guide gives temperatures in both Fahrenheit and Celsius but to convert from Fahrenheit to Celsius take the temperature, then subtract 32 from it and multiply the result by 5/9:

$$(Fahrenheit - 32) * 5/9 = Celsius$$

We've listed out the temperatures from 37°C to 87°C which are the most commonly used range in sous vide.

Celsius	Fahrenheit	Celsius	Fahrenheit
37	98.6	64	147.2
38	100.4	65	149.0
39	102.2	66	150.8
40	104.0	67	152.6
41	105.8	68	154.4
42	107.6	69	156.2
43	109.4	70	158.0
44	111.2	71	159.8
45	113.0	72	161.6
46	114.8	73	163.4
47	116.6	74	165.2
48	118.4	75	167.0
49	120.2	76	168.8
50	122.0	77	170.6
51	123.8	78	172.4
52	125.6	79	174.2
53	127.4	80	176.0
54	129.2	81	177.8
55	131.0	82	179.6
56	132.8	83	181.4
57	134.6	84	183.2
58	136.4	85	185.0
59	138.2	86	186.8
60	140.0	87	188.6
61	141.8	88	190.4
62	143.6	89	192.2
63	145.4	90	194.0

SOUS VIDE THICKNESS TIMES

For more Cooking by thickness information you can view our equipment section on our website where we have an iPhone thickness ruler and free printable thickness cards.

You can find them on our website here:
http://bit.ly/e7Lth2

There are two ways to cook sous vide, one is based on the thickness of the food and the other is based on the desired tenderness.

Cooking based on thickness is how PolyScience, Baldwin, and Nathan started out as they did research on food safety. Cooking sous vide based on thickness basically tells you the minimum time you can cook a piece of meat to ensure it is safe and comes up to temperature in the middle. It doesn't take into account tenderizing time or any other factors. It's often used by restaurants or home cooks who want to minimize cooking time and are using tender cuts of meat that don't need the tenderization.

Cooking sous vide based on tenderness takes into account how tough a piece of meat is and how long it needs to be cooked in order to make it appealing. So a chuck steak needs to be cooked a lot longer than a filet, even though they are both safe after the same amount of time. As long as the minimum cooking time is met for the temperature used, then it's completely safe to eat.

Both sous vide methods have their uses. Thickness-based is great for very tender cuts cooked by people who need them done in the minimum amount of time. Tenderness-based is best for tougher cuts or people that have a range of time that they are interested in.

A Few Notes on the Times

Times were extrapolated from the descriptions in Baldwin's Practical Guide to Sous Vide (http://bit.ly/hGOtjd) and Sous Vide for the Home Cook, as well as Nathan's tables on eGullet and a few other sources. (http://bit.ly/eVHjS3).

The times are also approximate since there are many factors that go into how quickly food is heated. The density of the food matters a lot, which is one reason beef heats differently than chicken. To a lesser degree where you get your beef from will affect the cooking time, and whether the beef was factory raised, farm raised, or grass-fed. Because of this, I normally don't try to pull it out at the exact minute it is done unless I'm in a rush.

The times shown are also minimum times and food can be, and sometimes needs to be, left in for longer periods in order to fully tenderize the meat. If you are cooking food longer, remember that food should not be cooked at temperatures less than 131°F (55°C) for more than 4 hours.

Heat from Refrigerator to Any Temperature

How long it will take to heat an entire piece of meat from 41°F / 5°C to the temperature of the water bath.

Reminder, this food might not be pasteurized at these times and food should not be cooked at temperatures less than 131°F / 55°C for more than 4 hours.

While there are slight differences in the heating time for different temperatures of water baths, the times usually vary less than 5 to 10% even going from a 111°F / 44°C bath to a 141°F / 60.5°C bath, which equates to a difference of 5 minutes every hour. We show the largest value in our chart, so if you are cooking it at a lower temperature you can knock a little of the time off.

Heat from Freezer to Any Temperature

How long it will take to heat an entire piece of meat from 32°F / -18°C to the temperature of the water bath.

Reminder, this food might not be pasteurized at these times and food should not be cooked at temperatures less than 131°F / 55°C for more than 4 hours.

While there are slight differences in the heating time for different temperatures of water baths, the times usually vary less than 5 to 10% even going from a 111°F / 44°C bath to a 141°F / 60.5°C bath, which equates to a difference of 5 minutes every hour. We show the largest value in our chart, so if you are cooking it at a lower temperature you can knock a little of the time off.

Pasteurize from Refrigerator to 131°F / 55°C

This is the amount of time it will take a piece of meat that is 41°F / 5°C to become pasteurized in a 131°F / 55°C water bath.

Pasteurize from Refrigerator to 141°F / 60.5°C

This is the amount of time it will take a piece of meat that is 41°F / 5°C to become pasteurized in a 141°F / 60.5°C water bath.

Heat from Refrigerator to Any Temperature

70mm	6h 25m
65mm	5h 30m
60mm	4h 45m
55mm	4h 0m 0s
50mm	3h 15m
45mm	2h 40m
40mm	2h 10m
35mm	1h 40m
30mm	1h 15m 0s
25mm	0h 50m
20mm	0h 35m
15mm	0h 20m
10mm	0h 8m
5mm	0h 2m 0s

Heat from Freezer to Any Temperature

70mm	7 hrs 40 mins
65mm	6 hrs 40 mins
60mm	5 hrs 35 mins
55mm	4 hrs 45 mins
50mm	4 hrs 00 mins
45mm	3 hrs 10 mins
40mm	2 hrs 30 mins
35mm	2 hrs 00 mins
30mm	1 hrs 30 mins
25mm	1 hrs 00 mins
20mm	0 hrs 40 mins
15mm	0 hrs 25 mins
10mm	0 hrs 10 mins
5mm	0 hrs 02 mins

Pasteurize from Refrigerator to 131°F / 55°C

70mm	5 hrs 15 mins
65mm	4 hrs 45 mins
60mm	4 hrs 15 mins
55mm	3 hrs 50 mins
50mm	3 hrs 25 mins
45mm	3 hrs 00 mins
40mm	2 hrs 40 mins
35mm	2 hrs 20 mins
30mm	2 hrs 00 mins
25mm	1 hrs 50 mins
20mm	1 hrs 40 mins
15mm	1 hrs 30 mins
10mm	1 hrs 25 mins
5mm	1 hrs 20 mins

Pasteurize from Refrigerator to 141°F / 60.5°C

70mm	3 hrs 50 mins
65mm	3 hrs 25 mins
60mm	3 hrs 00 mins
55mm	2 hrs 40 mins
50mm	2 hrs 20 mins
45mm	2 hrs 00 mins
40mm	1 hrs 40 mins
35mm	1 hrs 25 mins
30mm	1 hrs 10 mins
25mm	0 hrs 55 mins
20mm	0 hrs 45 mins
15mm	0 hrs 35 mins
10mm	0 hrs 25 mins
5mm	0 hrs 21 mins

Pasteurize from Refrigerator to 135.5°F / 57.5°C

This is the amount of time it will take a piece of chicken that is 41°F / 5°C to become pasteurized in a 135.5°F / 57.5°C water bath.

Pasteurize from Refrigerator to 141°F / 60.5°C

This is the amount of time it will take a piece of chicken that is 41°F / 5°C to become pasteurized in a 141°F / 60.5°C water bath.

Pasteurize from Refrigerator to 146.3°F / 63.5°C

This is the amount of time it will take a piece of chicken that is 41°F / 5°C to become pasteurized in a 146.3°F / 63.5°C water bath.

Pasteurize from Refrigerator to 150.8°F / 66°C

This is the amount of time it will take a piece of chicken that is 41°F / 5°C to become pasteurized in a 150.8°F / 66°C water bath.

Pasteurize from Refrigerator to 135.5°F / 57.5°C

70mm	6h 30m
65mm	6h
60mm	5h 15m
55mm	4h 45m
50mm	4h 15m
45mm	3h 45m
40mm	3h 20m
35mm	3h
30mm	2h 35m
25mm	2h 20m
20mm	2h 5m
15mm	1h 55m
10mm	1h 45m
5mm	1h 40m

Pasteurize from Refrigerator to 146.3°F / 63.5°C

70mm	4h 0m 0s
65mm	3h 35m
60mm	3h 10m
55mm	2h 45m
50mm	2h 20m
45mm	2h
40mm	1h 40m
35mm	1h 20m
30mm	1h
25mm	0h 50m
20mm	0h 35m
15mm	0h 23m
10mm	0h 15m
5mm	0h 10m

Pasteurize from Refrigerator to 141°F / 60.5°C

70mm	4h 55m
65mm	4h 20m
60mm	3h 50m
55mm	3h 20m
50mm	2h 55m
45mm	2h 30m
40mm	2h 5m
35mm	1h 45m
30mm	1h 25m
25mm	1h 10m
20mm	0h 55m
15mm	0h 45m
10mm	0h 36m
5mm	0h 31m

Pasteurize from Refrigerator to 150.8°F / 66°C

70mm	3h 35m 0s
65mm	3h 10m
60mm	2h 45m
55mm	2h 20m
50mm	2h
45mm	1h 40m
40mm	1h 25m
35mm	1h 5m
30mm	0h 50m
25mm	0h 40m
20mm	0h 26m
15mm	0h 20m
10mm	0h 10m
5mm	0h 5m

Heat Fatty Fish to Any Temperature

These times show how long it will take to heat an entire piece of fatty fish from 41°F / 5°C to any typical temperature.

Reminder, this food might not be pasteurized at these times and food should not be cooked at temperatures less than 131°F / 55°C for more than 4 hours.

While there are slight differences in the heating time for different temperatures of water baths, the times usually vary less than 5 to 10% even going from a 111°F / 44°C bath to a 141°F / 60.5°C bath, which equates to a difference of 5 minutes every hour. We show the largest value in our chart, so if you are cooking it at a lower temperature you can knock a little of the time off.

Pasteurize Lean Fish to 131°F / 55°C

This is the amount of time it will take a piece of lean fish that is 41°F / 5°C to become pasteurized in a 131°F / 55°C water bath.

Pasteurize Lean Fish to 141°F / 60.5°C

This is the amount of time it will take a piece of lean fish that is 41°F / 5°C to become pasteurized in a 141°F / 60.5°C water bath.

Pasteurize Fatty Fish to 131°F / 55°C

This is the amount of time it will take a piece of fatty fish that is 41°F / 5°C to become pasteurized in a 131°F / 55°C water bath.

Pasteurize Fatty Fish to 141°F / 60.5°C

This is the amount of time it will take a piece of fatty fish that is 41°F / 5°C to become pasteurized in a 141°F / 60.5°C water bath.

Heat Fatty Fish to Any Temperature

70mm	6 hrs 25 mins
65mm	5 hrs 30 mins
60mm	4 hrs 45 mins
55mm	4 hrs 00 mins
50mm	3 hrs 15 mins
45mm	2 hrs 40 mins
40mm	2 hrs 10 mins
35mm	1 hrs 40 mins
30mm	1 hrs 15 mins
25mm	0 hrs 50 mins
20mm	0 hrs 35 mins
15mm	0 hrs 20 mins
10mm	0 hrs 08 mins
5mm	0 hrs 02 mins

Pasteurize Lean Fish to 131°F / 55°C

70mm	5 hrs 15 mins
65mm	4 hrs 45 mins
60mm	4 hrs 15 mins
55mm	3 hrs 50 mins
50mm	3 hrs 25 mins
45mm	3 hrs 00 mins
40mm	2 hrs 40 mins
35mm	2 hrs 20 mins
30mm	2 hrs 00 mins
25mm	1 hrs 50 mins
20mm	1 hrs 40 mins
15mm	1 hrs 30 mins
10mm	1 hrs 25 mins
5mm	1 hrs 20 mins

Pasteurize Lean Fish to 141°F / 60.5°C

70mm	6 hrs 30 mins
65mm	6 hrs 00 mins
60mm	5 hrs 15 mins
55mm	4 hrs 45 mins
50mm	4 hrs 15 mins
45mm	3 hrs 45 mins
40mm	3 hrs 20 mins
35mm	3 hrs 00 mins
30mm	2 hrs 35 mins
25mm	2 hrs 20 mins
20mm	2 hrs 05 mins
15mm	1 hrs 55 mins
10mm	1 hrs 45 mins
5mm	1 hrs 40 mins

Pasteurize Fatty Fish to 131°F / 55°C

70mm	5 hrs 15 mins
65mm	4 hrs 45 mins
60mm	4 hrs 15 mins
55mm	3 hrs 50 mins
50mm	3 hrs 25 mins
45mm	3 hrs 00 mins
40mm	2 hrs 40 mins
35mm	2 hrs 20 mins
30mm	2 hrs 00 mins
25mm	1 hrs 50 mins
20mm	1 hrs 40 mins
15mm	1 hrs 30 mins
10mm	1 hrs 25 mins
5mm	1 hrs 20 mins

Pasteurize Fatty Fish to 141°F / 60.5°C

70mm	6 hrs 30 mins
65mm	6 hrs 00 mins
60mm	5 hrs 15 mins
55mm	4 hrs 45 mins
50mm	4 hrs 15 mins
45mm	3 hrs 45 mins
40mm	3 hrs 20 mins
35mm	3 hrs 00 mins
30mm	2 hrs 35 mins
25mm	2 hrs 20 mins
20mm	2 hrs 05 mins
15mm	1 hrs 55 mins
10mm	1 hrs 45 mins
5mm	1 hrs 40 mins

MODERNIST COOKING RESOURCES

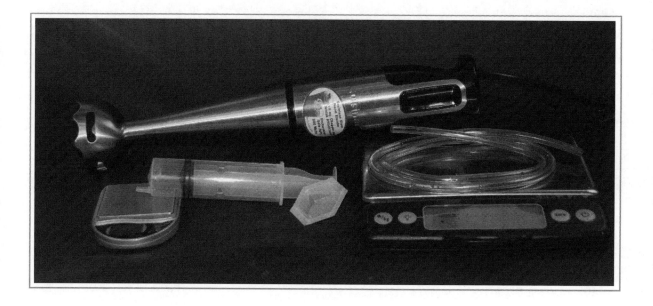

For an up to date look at current books, websites, and other modernist cooking resources you can visit the list we keep on our website.

You can find it at:
www.modernistcookingmadeeasy.com/info/
modernist-cooking-resources

Modernist cooking is a very complex process and there is much more to learn about it in addition to what has been covered in this book. There is more and more good information available about modernist cooking. Here are some resources to help you continue to learn more.

MODERNIST COOKING

Books

Modernist Cuisine: The Art and Science of Cooking

By Nathan Myhrvold

This aims to be the bible of modernist cuisine. It's over 2,400 pages costs $500 and was several years in the making. If you are serious about learning the newly developing modernist techniques then this might be worth the investment.

Modernist Cuisine at Home

By Nathan Myhrvold

A much more accessible version of Modernist Cuisine especially written for the home cook.

Alinea

By Grant Achatz

A beautify, picture filled book with amazing techniques and whimsical dishes.

Ideas In Food

By Aki Kamozawa and H. Alexander Talbot

Delve into the "why" of traditional and modernist cooking.

Texture - A hydrocolloid recipe collection

Compiled by Martin Lersch from Khymos.com, is a great compendium of recipes for many modernist ingredients.

On Food and Cooking

By Harold McGee

This is the ultimate guide to the scientific aspects of cooking. If you like to know why things happen in the kitchen, at every level, you will find this book fascinating.

Cooking for Geeks

By Jeff Potter

If you are interested in the geekier aspects of cooking then this book does a great job. It takes you through the basics of setting up your kitchen all the way up to kitchen hacks and sous vide cooking.

Websites

Modernist Cooking Made Easy

http://www.modernistcookingmadeeasy.com/

Our website is full of recipes, tips, and tricks for modernist cooking. We also have forums and other ways to talk with other passionate chefs.

Hydrocolloids Primer

http://www.cookingissues.com/primers/hydrocolloids-primer/

Dave Arnold and the Cooking Issues website help to clarify some of the uses of and reasons for modernist ingredients.

Apps

We also have an app for the iPhone and iPad available, as well as one for the Android. You can search in the app store for "Molecular Gastronomy" and ours should be near the top, published by "Primolicious".

SOUS VIDE

Beginning Sous Vide: Low Temperature Recipes and Techniques for Getting Started at Home

By Jason Logsdon

Our main book covering sous vide. It deals a lot with the various equipment options and has over 100 recipes, some of which have been specially adapted for this book. It is available from Amazon.com or on our website.

Sous Vide Grilling

By Jason Logsdon

Our book that is focused on grilling and BBQ recipes. It includes 95 great recipes covering steaks, burgers, kebabs, pulled pork, and everything in between. It is available from Amazon.com or on our website.

Sous Vide: Help for the Busy Cook

By Jason Logsdon

My book focusing on how to use sous vide around your busy schedule. Full of recipes, tips and tricks to make sous vide work for you.

Under Pressure

By Thomas Keller

This book shows you the extent of what is possible through sous vide cooking. The recipes aren't easy, and they require a lot of work but they can provide great inspiration for dishes of your own. If you are interested in expanding your concept of what can be accomplished through cooking then this is a must have.

Sous Vide for the Home Cook

By Douglas Baldwin

Baldwin helped to define and codify home sous vide cooking with his free online guide. His book is a nice intro to the subject, including food safety, and has many simple recipes to follow.

Websites

Cooking Sous Vide
http://www.cookingsousvide.com

This is the main website where I contribute sous vide articles. We update it regularly with original recipes and news from around the sous vide community. There are also community features such as forums and question and answer pages.

SVKitchen
http://www.svkitchen.com

A great site on sous vide cooking and one I read constantly. They touch on everything from standard sous vide swordfish to making your own preserved lemons with sous vide.

Sous Vide: Recipes, Techniques & Equipment
http://forums.egullet.org/index.php?showtopic=116617&st=0

A very long forum string from eGullet, about 98 pages long at this time that covers almost everything you need to know about sous vide if you have the time to look through it all. I suggest starting near the end and working towards the front.

Apps

We also have two apps for the iPhone and iPad available, as well as one for the Android. You can search in the app store for "Sous Vide" and ours should be near the top, published by "Primolicious".

INGREDIENT AND TOOL SOURCES

Many of the modernist ingredients cannot be picked up at the local grocery store. We have used several different vendors but we highly recommend Modernist Pantry.

Modernist Pantry
https://www.modernistpantry.com

Modernist Pantry has a good selection of ingredients and equipment. I tend to buy most of my ingredients through them. They blend a great service with good products and competitive pricing.

RECIPE INDEX

END NOTES

[1] For more details see http://en.wikipedia.org/wiki/Corn_starch

[2] For more details see http://en.wikipedia.org/wiki/Sugar#Refining

[3] Technically, they are called "phases", but I have tried to improve the clarity while sacrificing some specific scientific jargon. For a great in-depth look at how emulsions truly work, see: http://en.wikipedia.org/wiki/Emulsion

[4] For a detailed look at gels and fluid gels please see the chapter on Gelling.

[5] This is true of most gels, however, methylcellulose gels actually set above a certain temperature, not below it.

[6] I refer to these terms interchangeably, and for the home cook they really are. However, they do have some differences, especially in the academic vs industrial sectors and the full discussion of Thixotropy vs shear thinning is beyond the scope of this book. For an interesting look at it you can read the comments on the Wikipedia merge request: http://en.wikipedia.org/wiki/Talk:Shear_thinning

[7] This is definitely a simplification of the molecular processes. There are different ways this "mesh" forms, depending on the gelling agent and the liquid being gelled. However, the chemical processes behind this are beyond the scope of this book since we try to focus on the cooking aspects and less on the science behind them. There is a lot of good information on the internet that goes into much more detail about how gels really form in different situations.

[8] We discuss many of your options in our free online Beginning Sous Vide Guide (http://bit.ly/e8MvOu)

[9] Here is a good demonstration of the water displacement method: http://svkitchen.com/?page_id=296

[10] I have worked with all 3 of these companies in the past and most of the units were given to me as media demos. However, I have truly enjoyed using all 3 and recommend them to my friends with no reservations.

[11] We have done extensive testing of many sous vide units, for the results you can view our regularly updated sous vide equipment section. http://www.cookingsousvide.com/info/sous-vide-equipment

[12] http://www.amazon.com/gp/product/B0027HO3XO/ref=as_li_ss_tl?ie=UTF8&camp=1789&creative=390957&creativeASIN=B0027HO3XO&linkCode=as2&tag=primoliciousc-20

[13] You can view the data directly in the FDA's PDF: http://www.fsis.usda.gov/OPPDE/rdad/FSISNotices/RTE_Poultry_Tables.pdf

[14] In direct spherification you can use either calcium lactate or calcium chloride but because of the bitter taste of calcium chloride it is not recommended in reverse spherification because it is in the liquid, not the setting bath.

[15] I'm referring to real vanilla extract, not the common imitation extract that is chemically produced.

[16] The freeze-thaw and gel clarification techniques are beyond the scope of this book but in brief, they use the leaking of liquid from the gels to easily filter liquids and create consumes. The liquid leaks out of the gel while the solids and impurities remain in it.

[17] I'm ignoring the effects of pressure on the water such as water boiling at a lower temperature at high altitudes since it still has a set point for the phase change.

[18] Ideas in Food have a website and book, both of which I highly recommend for both traditional and modern cooking tips and advice. http://blog.ideasinfood.com/

[19] For more information on fluid gels please see the Gelling chapter.

[20] You can find the article on Daniel's blog: http://danielrmoody.com/2012/01/08/powdered-vs-sheet-gelatin-converting-between-the-two/

[21] Lecithin can be used to make several types of foams, but commonly it is used to make airs. For a detailed look into foams and airs please read the chapter on Foams.

[22] For a more detailed look at direct spherification and reverse spherification please see the chapter on Spherification.

Made in the USA
Middletown, DE
25 June 2021